Musings
of Yesteryear

Musings
of Yesteryear

Bryce "Pete" Robertson

Ordering Information:

For orders and inquiries, please contact:
1-888-404-1388
www.goldtouchpress.com
book.orders@goldtouchpress.com

Printed in the United States of America

DEDICATION

This book is dedicated to all persons who have been diagnosed with Alzheimer's or any other disease that relates to cognitive impairment regarding memory loss. The author of this book has been diagnosed with the beginning of Alzheimer's. What I am aware of is that short term memory is one of the first signs of the disease. Although the future is cloudy, the past still glows with brilliance.

When my personal physician first revealed my diagnosis, I was asked to develop a philosophy of how I was going to proceed with my life. After much thought I responded with the statement that I had been an ordained clergyman for 56 years and that my confidence in my ability to serve the public had not waned significantly, therefore I would continue exercising my ordination as long as I felt I was being effective.

To speak of the future there is a limit to my ability, but to rehearse the past comes in encouraging flashes and with demanding clarity. The future is cloudy, but for the present the past is exceedingly clear.

So, journey with me, not into the future, but into the past when the journey was clear and promising. When the shadows of tomorrow are unclear and indecisive, the reservoir of yesteryear yields its treasure in great abundance. Follow me on a journey twice lived. Bryce Robertson

10 Warning Signs of Alzheimer

1. Memory Loss that disrupts daily life.
2. Challenge in planning or solving problems.
3. Difficulty completing familiar tasks.

4. Confusion with time or place.
5. Trouble understanding visual images or spatial relationships.
6. Mew problems with words in speaking or writing.
7. Misplacing things and losing the ability to retrace steps.
8. Decreased or poor judgement.
9. Withdrawal from work or social activities.
10. Changes in mood or personality.

CONTENTS

INTRODUCTION

The Reverend Allison Jean from St. Andrew United Methodist Church in Plano, Texas, was the preacher for chapel at Highland Springs one day. In the delivery of her sermon, she commented that many of us were "living in Lent when we should be living in Easter." (Permission was given to use her phrase.)

After much reflection, I began to think that her assessment was right on target. As I was preparing to release the manuscript of my memoirs to the publishers, I realized how relevant her statement was to the text I was about to have put into print.

As I have re-examined my life, I realized that for my first twenty-two years, I was desperately in search of something that only God could give me. I tried but could not achieve it on my own. I wanted to be good and to experience the better life, but I realized that it could not be earned; it could only be received. It took the Holy Scriptures and a kindly old preacher to make me aware of it. So what I hope to portray in this book is that the Lenten part of my life simply was the prelude that allowed God to open the door for me to invite Easter to enter into my life in a glorious way.

My mantra is as stated: "One cannot change the beginning; but one can start where he is and change the ending."

I had a very deprived upbringing. We lived in substandard housing all of my early life. We always had food on the table, but it was not the most nourishing or healthy. We were not "poor trash," but "they lived next door."

When I left home at eighteen years of age, I made a promise to my mother that when I came home from the navy, I would be a changed person, and thanks be to God, I came home ready and willing to have my life transformed. Through the miracle of grace, God made it happen.

CHAPTER 1

Tragic Origins

My story began years before I was born. I have chosen to begin with the birth of my grandfather and tell it forward from there. It is not a pretty story!

My paternal grandfather, Thomas H. Robertson, was born in 1818 in Kentucky. After the Civil War began, he joined the Tennessee Volunteers on April 10, 1861, in Edgewood, Tennessee, and was attached to Company C, Second Regiment. He was discharged in 1864. My grandfather's first wife, who had borne him two sons, died in Arkansas. He later married my grandmother, Martha Elizabeth Seminole Robertson, a full-blood Seminole Indian, in 1885. My grandparents had five children: four sons and one daughter. My father, born on April 2, 1891, was the youngest. Unbelievably, my grandfather was seventy-three years old when my father was born! My grandfather died eight days after my dad was born. I suppose he just couldn't take having another child at that age.

My father was to live a tragic childhood. Totally uneducated and unable to take care of her children, my grandmother farmed them out to neighbors who used the children as slave laborers. One's heart breaks for the poor, desperate woman in an age when there was no social aid; she did what she had to do. One's heart also breaks for the children who suffered from circumstances not of their own making and who had to live through it as best they could. As Dad told the story of his displacement at the age of four, his mother took him by wagon and mules several miles out into the country and left him with a stranger, an older woman he called Grandma Seah, and drove off with him running after the wagon until he became exhausted and fell. My dad told me nothing of his days with his guardian until he was old enough to begin learning a trade.

My dad developed an interest in carpentry. He rode a mule fourteen miles each way to visit a man who taught him how to cut rafters and other rudimentary tools of the trade. My dad followed the carpentry trade all of his life, mainly building single-family housing or remodeling older houses. Dad never learned the trades of plumbing, electrical work, or floor sanding. He always hired other professionals to do what he could not.

Dad was reared in Limestone County, Texas, in a small community named Farrar, twenty miles south of Groesbeck. He told me that his mother reclaimed him when he was older, particularly after he was learning a trade. She was exceedingly poor and needed support. Dad later moved to Crandall, Texas, where he met my mother. At the time of their getting to know each other, Dad worked in a drugstore. There are many things I never learned about my father. He rarely mentioned his early life and went for years at a time without seeing his mother. The first time I saw her, I was eleven years old. There was little or no affection between them. I think my dad went by to see her just to see his stepsister and an older brother. They were the only members of his primary family whom I ever met. There was no special recognition or affectionate greeting. It was almost as if a relationship never existed. I could hardly wait for us to leave.

My mother was of a different mold. She was born in Panola County in deep East Texas to an unusually loving and devoted family on September 12, 1890. Her parents were Robert Jasper and Nancy Jane Youngblood, who birthed four sons and four daughters. They moved to Kaufman County in about 1896 and settled in the town of Crandall. My grandfather had migrated from Resaca, Georgia, the site of a famous Civil War battle. My mother told the story that my grandfather crossed the Mississippi River on his sixteenth birthday on his trip to Texas. It was in Panola County that my grandfather met and married Nancy Jane Weir. It was a marriage of two Christian people who later reared their children in the faith, and all of them remained close to God and the church all of their days. My grandmother died an early death in 1899. My mother grew up with a single parent, assisted by an aunt who was a spinster. My mother was a strong believer and did her utmost to instill into her children a love for God and His church, to which she remained faithful all of her days. I believe to this day that my mother was my "patron saint" to whom I owe enormous gratitude for the life I have come to love, in service to my risen Lord.

CHAPTER 2

Memory,
One of God's Greatest Gifts

These are a series of early memories I faintly recall. The details are not clearly explained, but I have taken each one as far as I can under the limitations of age and the function of retention. I wish that I could supply more actual facts, but age and time have erased them from the glow of my childhood. I am positive that what I am writing is true, but many of the details have been washed out with time.

Earliest Memory

The earliest memory that I recall is not the date of my birth, July 10, 1930, but the day I can envision and recall in the walls of memory what was going on, which was the first time that experience recorded on my brain an event or person. Did it happen? Absolutely! Can I prove it? No. Do I need scientific evidence to show that it really happened? No. Then how do I know it really happened? I know it because I experienced it. The brain is one of the most remarkable organs God ever created. The brain has eyes of its own, with some kind of internal mechanism that can recall what one cannot prove, yet it records events and situations and preserves them for an indefinite period of time. Memory is like a photograph that fades with time until the images can no longer be seen or remembered. Memory is not hallucination. The first is based on fact, the other on perception and imagination.

I must have been about three years old. In my mind's eye, I can see my mother, probably in the kitchen and likely facing the cabinet that was against the back wall of the kitchen. I can see the inside of the house in which we lived. The only furniture I can see is a straight chair, like an old dining room chair, turned over, with the top of the chair and the front edge resting on the floor, and I was pushing the chair as if it were a plow, with my hands resting on the back two legs of the upturned chair. I was somehow mimicking my father with his hands on the handles of a Georgia stock, an early American plow.

Since I had no other toy, the chair occupied endless hours of my time as I was, no doubt, engaged in assisting my father in the tilling of the ground and the planting of the crops. In my mind's eye, I did this day after day and with great pleasure.

Faint Memory Enforced by Mother's Retelling

I do remember faintly the small country church where my family worshipped. I remember my mother telling me that, as a small boy, I did sing occasionally during worship, to her and the congregation's pleasure. Today, and as I was growing up, I cannot imagine doing as well as my mother thought I did. But who am I to say? My mother was a living saint to me.

Clear Memory—About Four Years Old

As the first step in the separation of our family, my older brother, Wayne, had earlier found a bride in one Gertrude McCormack and chose to stay behind near Gertrude's family. I remember a time when Wayne had come to get me in order for me to spend the night with him and Gertrude, who lived about two miles from my parents. I was very excited because it my first night to spend away from my parents.

When nighttime came, I was forced to sleep between Wayne and Gertrude because they had only one bed, but I was excited and felt safe being away from my parents. However, there was a slight complication—my brother was suffering from an itch. He was forced to get up every two hours to administer a compound to his body that consisted of a mixture of sulfur and kerosene, I think, or something that was repugnant to my nose. But something else was terribly wrong: I was feeling homesick and longed to be with my parents. To my surprise, and with great joy, my father came for me that next morning, announcing that my mother had baked me a cake. I could not wait to go home. It was my first feeling that "home is where the heart is."

Memory of Early Education

My most beloved friend when I was around the age of four was my sister, Frankie. She was about two and a half years older than me, and she began her first year in school in what must have been 1934. One of the earliest experiences in my life was that she homeschooled me her first two years in public school. Frankie would come home every day after school and teach me what she had learned that day. I always looked forward to it.

It was Frankie who instilled in me the joy of learning. I will forever be grateful to her for being the one who introduced me to books and learning in the early disciplines. Because of her, I was to expand my knowledge, which led me into a career that is priceless. There is something exciting about beginnings. People can go wherever their interests lead them and enjoy the journey immensely. Had I not become interested in learning and exploring the options for my life, I might have drifted into a most undesirable condition. Bless the memory of my sister, who initiated in me a desire for reading and searching for things that make for a better life.

Because of the early homeschooling and motivation from my sister, I experienced a rare phenomenon in the public schools. Because of her tutoring, my knowledge accelerated. I only spent four months in the first grade and then was promoted to the second grade at midterm. After the second term, I was promoted to the third grade for my second full year of school. When I first started in school, Texas had only eleven grades. When Texas developed twelve grades, students already in school were not penalized by having to go through twelve grades, so I was able to skip the eighth grade, meaning that I was able to graduate from high school when I was fifteen years old. I was too young, too immature, and without the resources to attend college even if I had been inclined.

But my gratitude goes out to my sister for encouraging me to become interested in education and for spending endless hours tutoring me, even though she was only a bit older than me. I think my early successes built within me a quest for knowledge that lingers with me still. How do I know? My memory confirms it!

CHAPTER 3

From a Flood to a Drought

In 1934, we lived on a farm between the small town of Crandall, Texas, and a community known as Warsaw, which was simply a community stop consisting mainly of a grocery store, a community school (all grades in one building), and a cotton gin. The farms were scattered throughout a territory known as Coleman's Bottom. It was rich farmland, and under ideal conditions, the crops were very productive.

In this particular year, devastating rains occurred north of our farm near the town of Rockwall. The rain was draining into the east fork of the Trinity River, which went through the end of our property. The force of the drainage burst the dams on the river, and our farm was flooded.

As a child, my parents took me down to where our crops were flooded, and I can still see the damage rendered. The cornstalks were perhaps eight feet tall, but water was at least two feet above their tassels. My parents were devastated by the disaster.

My older brothers were having fun swimming in the floodwaters, and I wanted very much to wade as well, but my parents apparently thought it was unsafe. I can only imagine what my parents were thinking: *What will we do? Where will we go? How can we afford to really do anything?* But my dad was a fighter—one who would tackle a chainsaw. I am sure that he came up with a solution that he thought was the best. My mother was never one to make suggestions, knowing my father's strong will. (Perhaps this trait was passed down to his children.) She was compliant and ready to do whatever he thought was best. Most of us are strong-willed and ready to move on. We are not always right, but we are always ready!

So my dad decided that we would move back to West Texas. He acquired (I assume he bought) a Model T truck, and all that we owned was no doubt loaded onto the bed of the truck. Away we went, with all of the older boys riding atop the furniture; only my sister and I were riding in the cab with my parents. I remember very little about the adventure, only that it was long for us and frustrating for my parents. I think my dad told me that gasoline was about ten cents a gallon. We probably had a few flat tires along the way. (We never went anywhere without a few flats). The number of days it took to drive the distance is unknown, but it was an exciting adventure for me.

Once we arrived in West Texas, I do not think it rained any measurable amount for the next several years, but we saw incredible sandstorms. Often, a storm would come out of the West preceded by dark black clouds, but the closer they came, they would begin turning reddish. And then the sand would blow, occasionally for two or three days.

On our arrival in Seagraves, my dad rented an abandoned lumberyard in which we could live. We moved into every available space possible that was under a roof and enclosed. The only thing remaining was the building where lumber had once been stored, which became the town playground, where children and youth would come and climb through the rafters and flooring where lumber had been stacked. My mother worried constantly that someone would get hurt. To her surprise, nothing ever happened.

Our living quarters were crude, but there was ample space for all. My dad could really pick our residences. Memory is simply a way to relive one's life, pleasant or not. For my family, it was usually not pleasant.

CHAPTER 4

Lumberyard to a Tent

I thought life in an abandoned lumberyard was kind of unusual, but it was nothing compared to where we lived next. The 1930s were not the best time for a family in West Texas, or anywhere for that matter. Some families lived a rather decent life, but my family did not fare well. We were poor, but as a child I was not aware of it. I thought surely it was the way most everyone lived.

Just before I started first grade, my family moved into a tent that was perhaps twelve feet by sixteen feet. It was the size that might accommodate a small family, but mine was anything but that. We understood what it meant to share. Let me explain. Twelve of us lived in this small place: my dad and mother, six boys, and one girl, in addition to the two older brothers' wives and the oldest brother and his wife's small baby.

We lived on a vacant lot at the edge of town. I do not think the rent was excessive, but the togetherness was extremely so. We managed somehow, and I survived to tell about it.

As I went through first grade, I never had much space to do my homework, but just think how many tutors I had! Most people would look upon that as horrible, but the truth is, I never gave it a second thought.

How was I to know? My dad was providing the best way he could. What did it hurt to sleep on a mattress on the ground between two older brothers? Did not everybody? Besides, I always slept warm. After all, this may have been preparing me for experiences yet to come—not necessarily the hardships that I have reported in the stories, but the impact of those hardships and how they would condition me for the years that lay ahead. I think as I looked back on the deprivations I experienced, I felt as if I may not have been as good as those who had been more fortunate. But I was a child of God, although I may not have like one.

But I have learned a great lesson: Life is not always fair, and deprivation is not a punishment. God loves each person equally, and He would not arbitrarily punish some and reward others. There has to be some positive benefit. For me it has proved itself over and over. I learned early to be a survivor.

For years I felt some shame because I was below the social level of my friends, but now I see it as a training ground for achievement. I would have never achieved what I have were it not for my humble beginnings. My early life gave me an incentive to achieve something worthy of being recognized and rewarded. I learned the hard way, and I learned early: "Life is hard by the yard, but by the inch it's a cinch!"

It was a short walk from the tent to my classroom, and I was always early. My successes in school made it better for me. I may not have been the smartest student in my class, but I was the quickest to respond to any question and the fastest one to solve a math problem at the blackboard. I was gaining confidence every day, and that was giving me an advantage in the classroom. One doesn't have to be poor to have a sister, but to have one like mine was worth it.

I don't remember much about living in the tent beyond what I have already mentioned, but I remember first grade and my teacher, Mrs. Sherrill. She was very strict, and I was a little restless in the classroom, if one wants to call it that. Furthermore, she was quick to paddle her students. I was, more than likely, over her knee more than any other student. She always paddled me with her hand and made it a practice to have all the other students laughing at the victim. It was a little embarrassing but not enough for me to stay off her lap. Looking back on it, I think I was a little bored attempting to learn what I already knew.

One day in class she called me to the front and said, "You and I are going to see the superintendent!" I was afraid of him because I had seen him whip other boys in the hallways or bathroom. So with fear and trembling I accompanied her to his office. As we went in and sat down, I was waiting for the worst.

She quietly said to the superintendent, "My student is wasting his time in my class. He already knows the first grade, and I want to recommend that he be promoted to the second grade at midterm," which was coming very soon. I do not remember the whole conversation, but the superintendent agreed, and within a few days I was a second grader. It seemed strange for me to get promoted at midterm, and the second graders seemed to resent it. But, strange as it may be, I was now one of them and competing alongside them. It may have felt strange, but it also felt very good.

CHAPTER 5

Tragic Fire: Move to Barn

One of the most tragic experiences in my parents' lives happened in about 1939. My dad had leased, to the best of my knowledge, a seven-room house about one-half or three-quarter mile just north of our town, Seagraves, Texas, on a small, sandy farm-to-market county road. I do not remember moving in, only living there. Our house was not on the school bus route, so we walked back and forth to school and town.

We had so much room that my dad subleased two rooms of the house to one family and two rooms to another family. A small orchard occupied either side of our yard, part of which he leased to a couple living in a small house trailer. Therefore, parts of three families lived in the seven-room house, while a couple occupied the small trailer home. One might say that my dad always made the most he could out of the least space. In our three rooms lived my parents, three sons, and one daughter. I never remember my mother complaining about anything. She seemed to always make the best out of bad situations.

I recall that we were awakened around three or four o'clock in the morning one day with a fire raging fiercely in the kitchen and dining area and moving swiftly throughout the other rooms. I feel certain the other tenants were experiencing rapid fire growth. My mother escaped the flames wearing only her gown, and my dad was wearing only his underwear. I had on a pair of overalls, my sister was in a cotton dress, my two brothers had only scant clothing, and a two-year-old nephew who was spending the night was in his nightgown. I have no recollection of what our neighbors were wearing, but I do remember the fire truck, which was unable to do anything because we lived about a half mile beyond the last fireplug.

My mother walked out perhaps a hundred yards or so behind the house to escape the onlookers. I am not sure what else happened that early Sunday morning. For a small child, it was the most excitement I had ever seen, but for my parents, it was the death of our home with all of its furnishings and personal memorabilia, disappeared forever.

The townsfolk came for hours on end afterward bringing bedding, tables, chairs, kitchen equipment—everything imaginable to enable us to convert our barn into a livable facility. We actually lived there for about a year and a half. When the sand blew, my mother needed to wash the dishes before we ate. It was not the ideal place to live for a few months, but we managed. It seemed this was our lifestyle—living in substandard dwellings.

A strange thing happened one day when we lived in the barn. My dad became what I thought was seriously ill. We sent for Dr. London, who came immediately. This was not the first time it had happened, and every time it did, I was petrified. Dad sounded awful. He moaned and groaned something terrible. I asked my mother, "Is he dying?" She sort of smiled and said, "No, honey, your dad is broke!"

I have wondered from my youth, what does it take to be an equal to other people? I was often embarrassed and wished that we were on the level of other people socially. I discovered later that it has nothing to do with social status, but the importance comes in the approval of the One who has created us. God places no one below another, but it takes time to wash that out of our systems. For me, it took a long time.

CHAPTER 6

The Most Difficult Years

When I have looked back over my life, I have tried to identify the most difficult times of my eighty-seven years. For me it was the times between 1938 and 1943. We lived on a farm about eight miles northwest of Seagraves, the nearest town.

The farm covered about 140 acres of sandy soil, which blew hard in the spring and yielded less-than-average crops. The house in which we lived was near an unpaved road, with some of the traffic being horse-drawn wagons. There were few automobiles then and some foot traffic.

Our house was of "box and strip" construction with no foundation. It simply was built on top of the soil. When the heavy rains would come, the water would wind its way around the sand dunes, enter our house through the back door, and go out the front. My mother would take things from the floor and put them on the beds, dresser, tables, and anything above water level. In West Texas, this much rain was rare.

We had an old barn in which we stored the corn and maize, or whatever we grew, that we usually fed to our animals. Whenever there was grass or weeds, the larger animals would feed on that. A fence surrounded the pasture to keep the animals from straying off. The farm produced very little other than food for the table, perhaps selling a little of feed grain or cotton. My dad brought money home from his work. We could have lived in the town and been as well off, but my dad was not a practical man and never shared his thoughts about much of anything.

The smaller animals, pigs, and chickens were kept in closer quarters, while the larger animals, like the cows and horses, were free to roam more widely because they were safer from the animals of prey.

Our farm produced water by way of a windmill. The water table was accessible by inserting a form of tubing that went one to two hundred feet below ground, and the water was drawn to the surface by wind power. The wheel had beveled blades that were turned by the wind, forcing a rod to move up and down with the insertion of a check valve that, when submerged in water, would lift the liquid to the surface and dump it into a barrel or watering tank.

The barrel would provide water for the household, and when the barrel overflowed, it drained into an earthen tank from which the animals could acquire their water. This is a sophisticated device, but it is also very simple in the way it provides adequate water. The water from underground was normally cold, which also provided refrigeration for keeping the milk and other ingredients cold.

This is man's use of nature to provide what humans cannot. The rest of farm life was maintained by the power of human effort, which produced sweat and muscle. To a young boy it was often boring and laborious. The time from sunup to sunset seemed like eternity.

Although I was in touch every day with God's good earth, I had not yet come to fully appreciate it. For me it was work, work, work. My only inspiration seemed to come from my mother, who was a godly woman who loved her youngest son very much. I received a great deal of inspiration from her loving touch and constant smile. Somehow I realized that to please her was all that I needed at the time. God was good, but it was shown to me through my mother. I wonder if she knows it was her faith in me that kept me going. At the time, my mother was the only God I knew. I have heard it said, "God could not be everywhere; that's why he made mothers."

What made the later years on the farm so unpleasant was the fact that my older brothers had gone to war and my sister worked in a restaurant in the nearest town. As I look back on it now, it probably was better for me than I thought it was then. I learned something about discipline that has enabled me to survive and find some measure of success in my older years. My father taught me, even though I resented it then, to never give up because some reward is around the corner.

Farm life was either hot or cold. The only thing that was constant was working sunup to sunset. When I worked in the field as a small boy, it was my job each morning to milk the cows, eat breakfast, and head to the field. We farmed with two large horses and a one-row cultivator or planter. Our horses were measured to be sixteen hands high, which made them very large. I could hardly get a bridle on them, for often they would raise their heads high when I was trying, and sometimes I would have to yell at them or kick them to get them to cooperate.

My mother had a signal when lunch was ready. She would go out behind the buildings and wave her apron, letting me know lunch was ready. I had the habit of starting my watch for her about one to two hours early. After every round I hoped I would see her. *No mother! Has she forgotten me? Never my mother!* When I was about to give up, there she would be. I would go in for lunch after I took the harnesses off the horses to allow them to rest before I went back out for the afternoon.

What made these years so difficult is that I was basically alone, a boy at the age of eleven to thirteen, working day after day with essentially no one to talk to or share life with. We were not meant to be alone. These were lonely years, miserable years, not because I carried the burden of the farm, but because I was basically alone.

In my older years, the lessons I learned were wisely used. When I grew older and changed my profession, I realized there were times I need to be alone. But then being alone had a greater purpose to it. I suppose there are lessons to be learned at times that seemed unfair and unrewarding. I know God's plan unfolds, but why did it have to take so long?

CHAPTER 7

The Move from Farm to Town

In the Fall of 1943, my family moved from the farm to the nearest town, which was Seagraves, Texas, a township of approximately two thousand residents. Seagraves was the primary shopping area for those who lived in a radius of three hundred square miles surrounding the township.

Seagraves had three grocery stores, two motion picture theaters, two drug stores, a small hospital with a staff of medical doctors, a cotton gin, two barber shops, a couple of small hotels, post office, several service stations, a few taverns, a bevy of churches and later a skating rink. The school district covered the breadth of the northern half of Gaines County. To me, as a child, Seagraves was the ultimate place to live, it was Main Street America.

The real "up-side" to being in town was no out-houses, windmills or kerosene cook stoves. We moved up 500 years in quality of life in one day! I must have toyed with the water faucets and commode half a day to make sure they worked properly.

Another thing, my Dad rented a house just a few blocks from Main Street. Instead of two hours with a horse drawn wagon I could hop-scotch down to Main Street in five minutes. Time seemed to whiz by instead of creep. My! My!

Another radical change I experienced was that every time I visited downtown, I wanted some ice cream, bubble gum or something else. I am sure that I "nickeled" and "dimed" my mother to distraction. It was then I heard a cry for employment, bluntly stated by my dad: "Pete, you need to find yourself a job!!" Thunder had sounded! My dad had spoken.

Why did he leave the farm? The noises on the farm were so pastoral, the cows mooing, the horses neighing, the chickens cackling, the coyotes howling – the sounds of nature being replaced by horns honking, automobiles clanging, all kinds of people noises, weird city noises that were loud and disturbing. Whatever happened to peace and quiet?

And then there were Saturdays! Farmers coming to town to park their wagons and horses on Farmers Lot the way we used to do. (How common?) The barber shops were busy (haircuts were .25$) The movie theaters were crowded entertaining the country folks with the likes of Buck Jones, Ken Maynard, Bob Steele and Lash LaRue plus the inevitable Saturday serial (thirteen weeks of a continuing saga, with all the great mystery being revealed in the final chapter.) There was always a cartoon and "coming attractions".

Oil was being discovered! Black gold they called it! Trucks rumbling down the streets bringing equipment for the new enterprises springing up all over the place. I couldn't believe that we had given up the quiet sounds of the windmills, the cows and chickens filling the air with the noises of nature, the winds rustling through the cottonwood trees for all this racket made by mechanical devices, and the endless sound of voices signaling that civilization has arrived and no more peace and quiet.

My dad had sold us out! Goodbye farm, animal sounds, night winds, endless chores-hello instant everything!!

Well Pete, tomorrow is the beginning of something new, and I have the feeling I am not going to like it, perhaps my dad will forget what he said. Are you kidding? My dad doesn't forget anything!

CHAPTER 8

My First Public Employment

Early one morning, after breakfast, I put on my only pair of "waist pants", a freshly ironed shirt, my only pair of "town" shoes and grudgingly made my way downtown, and walked the entirety of Main Street looking at all the businesses that our little town accommodated.

As I passed by each one, I was hoping the owner would come out and say: "Are you looking for a job? I really need someone your age." No such luck. I didn't know to approach anyone. Besides who would want to hire a thirteen-year-old anyway? If school would start, I would be spared the embarrassment of asking for a job.

After the morning had almost expired, I got up my courage to go into the Wacker's 5 and 10 cent store and asked to see the person who may be hiring. A tall lady with small beady eyes came up to me and said, "I understand you are looking for a job!" I said, "Yes ma'am." She looked me over and said "Well, I do need someone to keep the floors and windows clean. Do you think you can do that?" I told her I thought I could. She said, "come in tomorrow at 7:30am and I will give you a try."

I skipped almost all the way home to tell my mother I found a job! She was pleased and frankly I was a little scared. I was early the next morning and she introduced me to more brooms, mops and squeegees than I had ever seen, Then she laid out my work and my schedule as to how often I would sweep, mop and clean the windows and what areas I was to leave alone.

Frankly I had never touched any kind of equipment she had, besides most of it was heavier than I imagined it would be. But I kept my head down and feet moving most of the day. Before closing hours, I asked her if she wanted me to go over everything as she was closing. She did and I did, I went home that evening rather pleased about my first day's work.

The longer I worked there the more irritable the manager seemed to become. But the real catastrophe came when the manager hired two teenage girls as clerks. I was rather large for my age and, for some reason, felt it was my duty to make them feel welcome. So, I guess I spent a little too much time "visiting" with them, though fun it was.

Come Saturday evening, at closing time, the manager handed me my weekly pay. I thanked her kindly, but her eyes told me she was about to scold me. But to my surprise she smiled very sweetly and said to me: "Pete, I am not sure that this store can get by without you, but come Monday, we are sure going to try!" (Period)

CHAPTER 9

Employment Came Quickly

The next job came easily. Within a matter of a couple of days I was approached by an emissary of Mr. James Goodwin Thornhill, owner and operator of the Wallace Theater in Seagraves that, if I were available, he would like me to go to work for him immediately as the operator of the popcorn machine which I would operate by popping and distributing popcorn to as many persons (young or old) as entered the theater.

Not only would I distribute popcorn, I would also keep the box office windows clean, the lobby vacuumed and after the last showing of the evening I would have the distinct privilege of helping to sweep out the auditorium before we locked up and went home around midnight. (what a job description – and me being only thirteen years old). Oh! I could have all the popcorn I could eat and draw the healthy wage of one George Washington a day – 7 whole days a week. I could hardly wait to tell my dad.

So, the next day I reported to work early enough to master the popcorn machine before showtime. Everything went great the first day. Popcorn sales were brisk! Even some came back for refills (a no no to Mr. Thornhill). The projectionist was about 203 years older than me, but we made a compatible team.

There was a second theater on the other end of the block that had been closed because the town could not support two theaters. One occasional night my buddy and I would spend the night in the theater, sleeping on the carpet, often with two or three friends. (without the knowledge of Mr. Thornhill). As time passed, the oil boom brought more people to town and the second theater was opened. This was my first great promotion. I became the sole operator of the projector room at the Pix Theater in Seagraves, Texas with the "fat cat" salary of $17.50 per week.

The hours did not change, the days remained the same, but the salary ballooned! What changed was now I had to have the popcorn delivere4d to my station. The projection booth is noisy and very busy. One must continually be watching the screen, the "picture" must go on!

CHAPTER 10

My First Date

I had my first date when I was about fifteen. I had not planned it, although I had thought about it. I did not know who it would be, and I did not know when it would be. I was a little frightened to even think about it. Who would deliberately accept my invitation? I had been born in this town and knew most of the girls, but would they laugh at me if I asked them out? I did not know if I was trying to get up the courage or talk myself out of it.

Then, like a lightning strike, it happened! I didn't initiate it. I wasn't sure I was ready for it. I was excited but scared. But this was the way it happened, ready or not. A friend of mine named Tommy Oglesby caught me walking down the sidewalk, and he drove up and said, "Get in. Let's go out to the Lewellens' and see if we can get a date with the two sisters for Saturday night." It sounded like a swell idea, so I jumped into the car, my heart pounding in my chest.

We were about one mile out of town, and I began to get cold feet. "Tommy, do you really think we ought to do this?" It was so sudden! I had thought about dating for a long time, but was this the time? Why, I had the rest of my life! Had I been kidnapped to do it now? He seemed so confident about it all, but I felt so reluctant. I knew these sisters but not that well.

Perhaps they would be reluctant or even disappointed that we asked. A thousand questions came to my mind. What would I say? How would I approach them, much less their mother? Perhaps the desire to date suddenly overrode my fear.

When we arrived at their farmhouse, I was frozen in my seat. Tommy drove past the front door and around to the back door. Guests had to go through the kitchen into the dining room. Don't ask me why—that's just the way it was. When we pulled up to the kitchen door, of all things, Tommy honked his horn! I said, "Tommy, let's go!" He seemed as cool as a cucumber.

In a very short time, their mother came to the door and in a very raspy voice asked, "What do you boys want?"

I said, "Tommy, let's go!"

Tommy answered by saying, "We would like to talk with your daughters!"

The mother replied, "We don't provide curb service here. If you want to see my daughters, you will get out and come in!"

"Tommy, let's go!" I pleaded.

But Tommy opened the door, and I followed, petrified.

We followed her through the kitchen into the living room and were told, very gruffly, "You boys have a seat." I sat down on the nearest chair while she called the girls in. We acknowledged their presence. It was the first time I had ever seen them, and I wondered which one I would be dating. They were both cute, to my liking.

The mother quickly asked, "Where will you boys be taking them?"

Tommy responded, "To the Wallace Theater."

The mother responded, "Well, you had better be there because I make it a practice every once in a while to check on my daughters to see if they are where they are supposed to be."

Saturday evening, when we went to pick up the daughters, the older one said, "My mother never checks on us. We can go wherever we please."

I said, "We are going to the Wallace Theater!"

Before we had gone two hundred yards, my date leaned over and kissed me on my lips. I was utterly surprised but pleasantly pleased. My first kiss!

We went to the theater, as promised, but to this day I do not know what the movie was or who the stars were. It was still a successful date, in my opinion. We continued to date until I went into the navy, and when I came home on a ten-day leave after boot camp, I saw her every day. But when my leave was over, I did not see her for about two years.

In the meantime, my folks had moved to the Dallas area, and I learned that she had moved near Terrell. Through intense effort, I finally located her, and we dated during that leave period. I really think she expected us to get married and that I would take her back to California. I could hardly pay for the cigarettes I smoked, but I promised her I would write to her every day.

A few months after I had returned to my ship, I received an infamous "Dear John" letter from her stating that she had gotten married, which broke my heart. My caring shipmates told me the person she married was the mailman.

Thus ended the romance! I was broken hearted but lived to tell about it.

"Romance is often infatuation. Love finds its destination in your marriage partner!"

CHAPTER 11

Deer Hunting

I shot my first and last deer the year I turned fifteen. This is precisely how it all came about.

In the Fall of 1945, a few months after my fifteenth birthday, two brothers who owned a ranch South of Seagraves asked me if I would like to go deer hunting with them, in the Fall, out in New Mexico. I was thrilled to be asked and jumped at the opportunity.

The brothers were Hiram and Arch Brimberry whom I had known a couple of years. The brothers were both single and had purchased a few hundred acres and had contracted with my dad to build them a home, barn and corral on the property. I was working in a service station and whenever appropriate they would come in and fill their tanks with gasoline. They were personable and made me feel important.

When the time arrived for us to drive to New Mexico, the brothers informed me that they had several guns, saddles, bridles, etc. and that I would be able to use theirs. So, we left Seagraves with all their gear, plus warm clothing and drove to some place in New Mexico and spent the night.

The brothers were very entertaining. They knew how to make a boy of fifteen become one of them. I felt I had aged at least another fifteen years. Their conversation was decent, but they had a flare for the dramatic, but had a way of including me in the conversation. They respected my age but made me feel I was closer to theirs.

They left the light on in the room until the conversation was winding down, wanting me to feel that I was important enough to be included. Then, without any warning, Hiram grabbed his boot and broke out the ceiling light. "Goodnight" he said, and off to sleep, wondering what surprise lurked in the days ahead.

The next day we must have driven for six hours or more and we came to the township of Belen, New Mexico which was our final stop before we headed up into the mountains to a private ranch that was to host about eight adults and myself for several days. The Brimberry's had stayed there before and perhaps the other guests as well. The personnel that were employed by the owners included, to my best recollection was: The foreman of the ranch, perhaps two or three other men who were in charge of the horses and other visible property, a cook with a helper and I am not sure if there were anyone else.

The next day we were up early, breakfast was being prepared, and the day was mostly at leisure. The Brimberry's took me to the horse corral the next morning and supervised me in the selection of a horse for the length of time we would be there. My friends had purchased a hunting license for me. This day all of us at the ranch would take a horseback excursion up into the mountains, possibly as high as 9000 feet!

The mountain trails were narrow, and the mountain seemed to melt away from you as you rode the high ridges. I was taught to sit on the mountain side of the saddle, as the slope moved away sharply at times. The horses were a little jittery and frankly I was uncomfortably scared much of the time, ready to dismount on the mountain side if the horse slipped and fell down the mountain, I wasn't told this before I left home, as I may have stayed with my mother.

The day before the hunting season opened was exhilarating and informative. I learned a lot this day. There was a time that we left the horses tethered in a meadow and we walked what seemed like a long way, and in reality it was, in fact we ended up closer to the ranch house than we were to where we left the horses. So, we walked back to the ranch. Big problem, by this time it was nightfall.

The Brimberry's said to me, we will get you another horse and you can go with one of the stable boys and ride back up to where the horses are tethered. When you get there, take the bridle off the white horse and the horse will lead you back down the mountain trail to the headquarters. This was not to my liking one bit! The mountain air was cool, and the temperature was dropping slowly. There were all kinds of night sounds that warned me that dangerous animals were lurking nearby.

But on we rode, scared though I was, but I was committed to see this through. It must have been close to midnight when we had gotten back to where the horses had been left. I took the bridle off the white horse and turned him loose. The horse started off at a walk, then came a troy, and then the horse began to lead the other hoses back towards the ranch house. Of course, the ranch house had no visible lights showing from where we were. I estimate that we could be as far out as seven or eight miles. I was afraid the white horse might just take off running and I would be unable to stay up with him.

I have always heard the phrase "horse sense", but now I was seeing it beautifully demonstrated. The white horse had been tested long before I had followed him, but the horse was experienced. He would not let the horses get too far behind, he would stop and wait. IO am not sure what time we returned to the ranch but probably three of four o'clock in the morning.

I may have forgotten the precise day when the hunting season was to begin, but whenever it was, we were on the trail long before sunup hoping to be in the higher elevations whenever we may be able to spot a deer. The sun had been up perhaps an hour or so, when someone spotted a deer some 200-300 yards away. All of the men scrambled for their guns, but Hiram said: "Wait! I want Pete to take the first shot. If he misses, it's anyone's deer."

I got off my horse and got my gun out of the scabbard and took aim. The deer was a trophy animal standing broadside to me. Hiram had told me that to properly kill a deer was to shoot him in the shoulder. Never shoot a deer in the head; it would mess up the animal if you wanted to mount the head on a trophy. I was on my knees with the crosshairs of my sight about two feet above its knees, in the lower part of the shoulder. I fired and the deer went down. The hunting party hurried to the spot where the deer lay, wounded but not dead. Hiram took a large knife and slit the throat of the animal and allowed it to die.

I must have been shaking fiercely, with all the hunting party congratulating me. It was an 8-point buck, a trophy indeed. The men put the dead animal on my horse behind the saddle. Hiram told me to take the deer back to the ranch and have one of the men dress it for me. There was a large tree near the house where he hung the deer and immediately dressed it. Mine was the only kill the first day. I felt like a million. A beautiful 8-point buck which dressed out a bit over 130 pounds.

CHAPTER 12

A Promise Made, A Promise Kept

I grew up in a rather dysfunctional family, beginning with my father. His parents' child-rearing style, which I have already written about, caused some serious disorders that were too difficult for him to overcome. His early life was extremely traumatic. I mentioned that he was given away at about the age of four. Being reared away from his mother and his siblings was extremely difficult. My father never went through analysis, but his personality exhibited severe abuse.

The way my siblings were raised had a negative effect on most of them as well. I do think that each one of them had the opportunity to alter their lifestyle, but three or four of them did not until they became older. This is not a condemnation of any of them, but it is an observation that there was perhaps an experiential tendency to walk a line a little awkwardly, especially when they were younger.

Examples are unnecessary. All one has to do is study family history to determine for oneself. As the family members became older, their conduct became much better, with a couple of exceptions. I do not wish to exclude myself, but I did live a more disciplined life than most.

One thing made a distinct difference in my life. I made a promise, and by and large, I kept it. Let me explain the nature of the promise and the vow I made to keep it. I had four brothers in WWII, a vicious war. Many were killed, and many more were wounded. A great deal of pressure was placed on those who saw action. Two of my brothers were involved overseas, and they saw a great deal of action. One was wounded, perhaps more than once. What we now know as posttraumatic stress disorder could have been their experience or something worse.

The other two saw no action, but perhaps the stress of the war and the possibility of their involvement created some kind of unfavorable disorder. However, all four became much better adjusted as they aged.

This story is not intended to denigrate my brothers or to make me look good; it is the making of a promise that was not an oath to God but, in actuality, an oath to my mother, who was the nearest thing to God in my life at the time. How else can I say it? It was a sacred moment to me! What else could it be? I made a promise to her that I would not come back from the military in the conditions that my brothers exhibited. When I walked out of the gate after I was discharged, I remembered the promise and said to my navy friend who also had been discharged, "Mel, from here on I plan to live the way I promised my mother—no more alcohol. My wife and I plan to join a church and change our habits to which I have become accustomed these past four years. I am newly married, and I want to establish a home in which we can rear children who come to know the Lord." Goodbye, navy! Hello, civilian life!

CHAPTER 13

My Quest for Adventure

I joined the Navy to see the world and I have not been disappointed. My travel experience before the Navy was very limited. There was an occasional visit to a relative but that was the limit of my experience. I longed for more, much more. I wanted to see those places most talked about, where the privileged wanted to go.

When I was a teenager, there was a song at the top of the charts that went something like this; "Those far away place3s – with those strange sounding names…are calling…calling me!" I longed desperately to visit them. The only way I was likely to visit them was to let Uncle Sam pay the freight. I seemed born for this purpose.

After "Boot Camp" I was transferred to Long Beach, California to await the arrival of the ship to which I had been assigned. I knew nothing about her except that she had been on a tour of the Far East. My expectations were unlimited. But wait I would, enjoying the simple pleasures of Southern California.

I was housed in temporary quarters, dreaming of the future by day and enjoying Long Beach by night. The monotony was somewhat boring. Then one evening as we approached the gate to go into Long Beach for our daily amusement, the Shore Patrol stepped in and informed us that there was a "forest fire" in Topanga Canyon, north and west of Los Angeles. We were advised to return to our barracks building, put on our dungarees and report to a bus that would take us to our destination. We were told; "Tonight, all of you will play Forest Rangers!"

A bus carried about thirty of us into the canyon and turned us over to the command group who put us to work clearing brush and digging trenches for whatever. Periodic refreshments were served.

The night was long, and the work was hard, but there was a reward built into the effort. Besides, I would probably never have had the experience of a Forest Ranger.

The remainder of the time on the Naval Base went very well. The time gave us the opportunity to explore the Los Angeles area. The better transportation into L.A. was the street cars (electric) and, if necessary, one could transfer to a bus that would deliver you to more specific locations. Also, a plus, all the major motion picture companies had large, beautiful theaters.

Long Beach itself had "The Pike", a recreational area near the beach. There was a Ferris wheel, and small boats one could rent to take your date on the lagoon! There were other amusement rides and games, restaurants and sooner or later you would run into a friend.

But the thrill of a lifetime, what I had been waiting for had finally arrived! A harbor tug was bringing the largest ship I had ever seen into a pier. My heart was pounding in my chest! There it was #75 painted on the bow. The U.S.S. Helena itself, my new home. I rehearsed the numbers in my head; 684' long, 80' wide – a man-of-war ship with three 8" turrets, 6 5" mounts, 13 40mm gun placements-what an awesome sight!

The number of crew members was approximately 1400 officers and enlisted men – almost as many who lived in Seagraves, Texas. I went aboard at the proper time assigned to the "Fox" division. I was taken to a compartment, assigned a bunk and a locker. Our sleeping quarters were a mite crowded, sleeping three and four deep from bulkhead to bulkhead.

It will take a while to meet and great all my buddies. Everyone has been "Texas" friendly. One of the funny stories (true) is that I had to have an escort for a few days in order to find the chow hall and my way back to my bunk.

My quest for adventure had been answered. My pleasure craft was moored in Long Beach, Ca. My reason to be had yet to find an answer – but my quest for adventure was now impart every time it set sail – my heart went kaboom.

CHAPTER 14

Pre-Navy Years

Growing up on a sandy land farm in West Texas, I appeared an unlikely candidate to join the navy. What did I know about water? I had seen so very little in my life.

I had four brothers in World War II. One was in the cavalry, one in the army, and two in the air force. All of them survived, for which I give thanks.

Early in 1948, two friends of mine from my hometown—we will just call them Marlin and Red—encouraged me to go with them to Abilene, Texas, in order to join the navy. I had always wanted to see the world, and this appeared to be my chance. My parents were agreeable, so off we went, excited about a new adventure. When we arrived in Abilene, we went to the recruiting station to enlist. We were told that in order to join the navy, we had to be eighteen years old. Two of us were seventeen, and we did not have a permission slip from our parents.

Then, a bright idea came to our minds! Why not go to Houston and join the merchant marines? We boarded a bus headed to Houston very excited about our new plans. Different service, same ocean! When we arrived in Houston, we went immediately to the recruiting office, not knowing the requirements. Again, we were told the same story—we had to be eighteen years old.

We had come to the end of the line, and we had run out of money. There we were, "landlubbers" in a foreign land, with no money. One of the boys telegraphed his mother asking her to wire him some money, which he said he would share with us. We waited near the telegraph office for what seemed an eternity without results.

We huddled to see if we could come up with the next brilliant idea. After a short time, we decided to hitchhike from Houston to Amarillo because the other boy with us had two sisters and a brother in Amarillo from whom we could sponge for a few days. (It is desperate to be penniless in a strange land.) So we caught random rides back out to the edge of Houston to begin our endless job of begging for rides. We stood with our thumbs out for a couple of hours with no luck. Then, bingo! Marlin made one last call to the telegraph office. His mother had wired him the money.

We spent our last few shekels for bus fare back downtown, picked up the money, and bought bus tickets to Amarillo. It was perhaps an eight-hour journey. Once there, we were among friends and family. Panhandling among Red's family was easy and lucrative. We spent about a week there enjoying the hospitality of old friends.

But as all good things do, the party came to an end and it was time for us to head back home. This was my first adventure without my parents. I was being led by a group of my peers, and I discovered very quickly that we lacked the maturity to make the right decisions. Being wrong isn't right; however, it seemed fun to a boy of seventeen.

Back home, I was safe and sound in my mother's bed, yet I still was preoccupied with wanderlust. Why had everything gone wrong? I knew where I wanted to be, but I could not see how to get there. But within a couple of months, I was approached by two boys from a very small town east of Seagraves who wanted to join the navy and asked me to join them. I was within days of turning eighteen and more than ready to join the navy and "see the world."

A few days later, we went to Lubbock, Texas, and visited the navy recruiting station, where we met two other boys—one from Lubbock and the other from Levelland—and we five were sent to Albuquerque, New Mexico. There, we were sworn in on my eighteenth birthday, July 10, 1948. We were then given tickets to catch a train, with sleeping berths, bound for the Naval Training Center in San Diego, California. I felt for the very first time that I had matured from a boy into a man.

From Albuquerque to Los Angeles, we would take on other recruits at every stop. By the time we reached Los Angeles, we must have had three hundred naval recruits or more. In Los Angeles, we had a two- or three-hour layover before they boarded us on the oldest train I had ever seen. All of the seats were wooden, and the trip to San Diego was mountainous, at least for that train. I shall never forget that we were going up one long hill, huffing and puffing as if we were about to come to a stop. To our amazement, we were going through a beautiful orange orchard. I do not know who started it, but suddenly all of the recruits began leaving the train, running through the orange grove and filling their pockets and shirts with oranges. I found myself among the pack, huffing and puffing to catch the train before it reached the top of the hill. I have no idea what we did with all the oranges we took from the orchard, but it was an exhilarating experience as my heart pounded wildly in my chest.

When we arrived in San Diego, we departed the train and boarded buses in groups assigned by some enlisted men who looked like we wanted to look in a short period of time. We were transported to the Naval Training Center, assigned to a company, and marched to our barracks. It was our good fortune that all five of us were assigned to company 291 and were bunked very close to one another.

The next morning, we were loosely marched over to the naval clothing center and given our uniforms, most of which fit us to some degree. I was a very skinny, 145-pound, 6-foot, 2-inch young man. My clothes fit me rather loosely. I could gird my canvas belt as tightly as I needed to hold my pants up. I was very proud to receive my uniform, especially my dress blues. We were restricted to base for the first three weeks, and then we were given liberty from 5:00 p.m. until midnight, only on weekends, for the next thirteen weeks.

The second morning of our boot training, we were marched over to the base barber shop for our initial haircut. I was in an eighty-man company, and I believe it took about thirteen minutes for six barbers to cut all eighty men's hair. Many of the men cried when their curly locks hit the floor. In thirteen minutes, we all looked like sheep that had been sheared. It was not a beautiful sight. Since it was July when I was inducted and the naval base was near the ocean, our heads blistered something awful.

One of my pleasant surprises came at the rifle range. We were using M-1 rifles trained at a target perhaps two hundred yards away. A person spotting would either wave us off, saying what in navy jargon would be a word not used in everyday speech to mean that we had missed the entire target or would give some signal that you we had hit the target with some accuracy. I was pleased to come in second place out of eighty men. My original targets on the farm were rabbits, hawks, or rattlesnakes, but my early use of a rifle paid off.

When I was given my first liberty to go into San Diego, I went with the rest of my famous fivesome, all of us in our dress blues. One of the first mistakes I ever made was with the other members of our group: we went into a tattoo parlor, and each of us had the same tattoo put on our lower left arms. The tattoo was an eagle with spread wings, and in the space across his legs was written, "U.S. Navy." All of it covered a five-point star with the word "Texas" written on it. It proved to be painful and bloody but cool. What I did not exactly know then is that when you get a tattoo, it is forever. That event happened seventy years ago as of July 10, 2018.

Much more will be told about my navy career over the next few pages.

CHAPTER 15

Induction into the U.S. Navy

July 10, 1948 introduced me into the most exciting time of my life, to date, because it was my eighteenth birthday and the day, I was enlisting in the United States Navy, at the recruiting station in Lubbock, Texas.

At the time I was inducted, I was accompanied by four other young men my age who were to join me in the ceremony. Two of the men I was well acquainted with because they were from a small farming community 8 miles East of my hometown. Their small community was comprised of perhaps two hundred residents. The community was known as Loop, which had their own public school, with the only modern gymnasium in a radius of 30 miles.

These two men from Loop were good friends of mine, one being W. H. Brewer and the other Johnny Day. One of the four was William Gorman from Brownfield, Texas and the other was Rod Cameron from a small town near Lubbock. We easily meshed into inseparable "buddies". This was big time stuff and we were glad we had been brought together for this singular purpose.

The five of us strode the streets of Lubbock until late night when we were told to report to our hotel. We were up for an early breakfast before reporting to the recruiting office for the day's schedule. We were given a pep talk before we boarded a train for Albuquerque, New Mexico where we would actually be sworn in. We were five proud men knowing that we would make Uncle Sam good seamen.

We were minor celebrities on the train. Feeling our "oats" and I am sure entertaining (or boring) the passengers. We loved the train ride and spent most of the day getting better acquainted. As far as we knew there were no other recruits on the train.

We arrived in Albuquerque and were transported to the recruiting station. We were placed in a clinic and were stripped of our clothes in a large room. (I felt very uncomfortable but said to myself: "Get used to it!"). A doctor came in and gave each of us a physical exam (my first). He pronounced us fit and allowed us to get dressed. We then were actually sworn in. I was no longer a civilian from Seagraves, Texas, I was a member of the U.S. Navy…and proud to be so.

The after spending another night in Albuquerque we were placed on a train, complete with Pullmans and dining cars. We five all bunked close to each other with perhaps a few other recruits we picked up in Albuquerque. The trip from there to Los Angeles took two overnights. I had never slept in a pullman before, and this made me look forward to a bunk on a ship somewhere in the Pacific.

We picked up several recruits on our way to L.A. When we pulled into Grand Central Station, we must have had 300 or more recruits.

Before we arrived in Los Angeles, I had noticed the terrain had changed noticeably. No more desert and scrub brush along the way, now there were palm trees and beautiful flowers. The grass was green, and the air had become a cool soft breeze. The sun was shining, and I was enthralled with the flora and fauna of Southern California.

The military escorts gathered all the recruits together and told us to stay in the area of the train station until our train arrived to carry us to the San Diego Naval Training Center, which would be our home for the next three months.

We must have waited for two or three hours until our train was announced. We were herded along to whatever track our carriage awaited. But there it was! In regal splendor! I could not believe my eyes. There in the track sat the oldest passenger cars I had ever seen! A smoky engine and several passenger cars right out of the 1900's. Wooden seats to the last car. They must have carried the miners to the California gold rush.

Quickly we were loaded onto the antiques and began huffing and puffing heading South at a clip of 5 of 6 miles per hour until we got out into the open tracks and then we moved up to perhaps 15-20 mph.

I joined the Navy for this? For all I knew I might be shipping out on wooden ships.

Then when we had gotten about halfway to San Diego, we started a relatively steep upgrade through the middle of an orange orchard. We must have slowed to a walk when all the sudden the passengers of the train disappeared out into the orchard stuffing oranges into their pockets and putting them inside their shirts. Within minutes the train unloaded all passengers and continued its climb to the top of the crest. Judgement was "how many oranges can I gather and get back to the train before it topped out?" (As far as I know we lost nary a man).

(That was the last time I have ever pilfered fruit out of someone's orchard.)

When we arrived at the Naval Training Center we were kept together and placed into eighty-man companies. All five of the Texas boys were able to be in the same company (Company 280). Our company was separated from the rest and loosely marched to our barracks building and we five Texans were allowed to choose our own bunks. (Naturally we chose to stay together). After "chow call" we bunked down for the night.

The next morning my company 280 was herded over to the base barber shop and given a haircut – not our choice but theirs – all offed – skinned!! There was weeping and wailing and gnashing of teeth! The first time I had seen so many grown men cry! When most had gained some composure, we were taken to clothing" and each of us were fitted with our entire wardrobes. (Some came close to fitting.) So, I put on Navy clothing for the first time. Navy dungarees, a far cry from dress blues or whites. We were told that it would be three weeks before we were allowed to go into San Diego. (big deal – it took months for my hair to grow out enough to comb. On top of that my head blistered.)

The next morning, we met our company Commander, who would be our drill instructor for the next three months. His name has long since been forgotten, but he was a Chief Petty Officer – a survivor from the aircraft carrier, sunk in the Pacific during the war. Unlike the Marine Corp he was neither loud nor exceedingly demanding. He expected excellence from his company, but I found him to be patiently humane and respectful of his men. Because of that, we had good rapport and little dissention in our ranks.

1948 was the year President Truman integrated the military. Our company had two African American men assigned to its ranks. Integration, as I remember it went smoothly after many questions, but none resisted.

Then came our first liberty! We dressed in our finest and eager to go ashore, although we had been ashore for three weeks, but we had to think like a sailor. Once we were ashore, we five Texan's decided to get a tattoo. All of us agreed to get identical tattoos engraved on our left forearm. The configuration was a Texas Star, with the spread of Eagle's wings and U. S. Navy printed as a scroll across the top and the word Texas across the bottom.

I was so excited to follow Navy tradition by getting a tattoo! My mother would be so proud of me. I was feeling my "oats" until he turned on a handheld outliner making lots of racket and spewing blood all over the place. What have I done? Sacrificed my life for the sake of Texas! Half crying and half laughing I thought the kingdom had come – amid a blood bath! What will my mother think now?

CHAPTER 16

My First Cruise -
Pollywog to Shellback

My first real cruise (I was so excited) came early in 1949. It might not have been for pure pleasure, but it was welcomed by me. At last, we were going to sea.

As we left Long Beach, the ships compass was pointed southerly in the direction of the Panama Canal. Perhaps the rumors were right for a change. We did not know the full itinerary, but the rumor has it that we would cross the Equator somewhere near the Galapagos Islands, home to the large sea turtles.

When we left Long Beach a few crew members built a large canvass tank on the fantail of our ship with dimensions of something like 14' square and perhaps 10' deep. Each day the mess cooks would dump garbage into the tank. Could it be...? There was a foul odor and many suspicious suggestions.

Finally, the day arrived. We were told the ancient story of King Neptune Rex and his side-kick Davy Jones. So, we sailed around the Galapagos Islands and the ship came to an absolute stop just above Rex's throne on the equator.

The ship cut all engines and a "boom" was swung out at mid-ship. Ladders were lowered over the side and word was passed that anyone wanting to swim in the "brinny-deep" were welcome to do so. Then the long awaited and dreaded announcement was made: "Beginning at 9:00am the next day, the initiation of the "Pollywogs" would begin (referring to all naval personnel, including the ship's captain, if they had never crossed the equator before aboard a Navy vessel).

All Pollywogs will appear at the bow of the ship promptly at 9:00am. The dress for the day will be white pants only. (no hat, shirt, socks, shoes or underwear, etc.) So early the next morning all crew members to be initiated were lined up from the bow down the side of the ship almost to the fantail, ready to crawl on hands and knees the entire length of the ship, with the Shellbacks peppering each Pollywogs posterior with canvass whips. Any complaining by the Pollywog received extra compensation.

King Neptune Rex had as his guests such demons of the deep as Davy Jones, her highness Amphitrite (goddess of the deep), the Royal Scribe, the Royal Doctor, the Royal Dentist, the Royal Baby, the Royal Navigator and the Royals – Chaplain, Judge, Attorneys, Barbers and others who may suit the Kings Court.

The Pollywogs were brought singly before members of the Royal Family and were punished in some form (minors). The initiation lasted the better part of the day. There was fun for all and punishment (mild) for a few. At the end of the ceremony, every Pollywog was placed in a chair with his back to the canvass garbage tank and flipped high in the air over backwards into the tank. Once you made your way out of it, you could go take a shower and then to the dining room for dinner.

Sounds gross! It was, but no-one was injured – fun was had by all. We returned home as Shellbacks!

P.S. This was my first major cruise. The ocean was beautiful, the skies clear, winds were calm, and the waves were minimal. I was initiated and became a Shellback (with papers and all) but never crossed again as a Shellback to initiate other Pollywogs.

CHAPTER 17

First Hawaiian Voyage

After arriving back in Long Beach following an unforgettable voyage across the Equator with the ancient naval ceremony of being transformed from a Pollywog into a Shellback. The ship went through an extensive overhaul to "ready it" for future voyages.

I was overjoyed when we set sail for the Hawaiian Islands, which was very high on my "Bucket List". I had seen movies filmed in the islands and was simply ecstatic to learn within a few weeks I would probably be walking on their beaches.

On the day of our arrival, my ship was routed around Pearl Harbor. The year was 1949. AT the entrance into the harbor a pilot came aboard the ship, while a large tugboat was secured to our vessel. After assuming the control of the movement of our ship, he began describing what happened on December 7, 1941, "the day of infamy".

He began his lecture with the first wave of Japanese planes, both bomber and torpedo, to initiate the destruction of our Pacific fleet. They had hoped to find the only two aircraft carriers America had in the Pacific and destroy them. Fortunately, the carriers were somewhere else in the Pacific, oblivious to their potential destruction.

Therefore, the premier targets were the Battleships moored side by side in an area known as Battleship Row! AT the time of the attack, the United States Navy had nine battleships in Pearl Harbor, eight of them were side by side, dead in the water. With bomber and torpedo planes pummeling them from the skies and water seven of the battleships were rendered useless and the battleship Arizona was permanently destroyed. A flag proudly waves over the remains which are a memorial to the proud men of service. I have visited the memorial on several occasions and offer a prayer each time for those who were killed in valiant courage.

We passed "Battleship Row" and other memorable sights before we dismissed the tug and were under our own power, we moved to the Waikiki area. We were able to secure a Pier at the Aloha Tower. As we were approaching the tower, we could hear the faint strumming of the Ukuleles with the familiar sound that introduced the Hula Dancers. Everyone was straining to see the dancers swaying to the sound of the music. (I thought I might die on sight).

Liberty was sounded at five bells, with liberty sailors moving swiftly across the deck to explore the beauties of Waikiki.

A trip to Waikiki in 1949 had little resemblance to the twelve times I have been back since I was discharged from the navy.

In 1949 the two hotels of prominence were the Moana and the Royal Hawaiian. There could have been many non-descript places to stay – but none with the distinction of those I named. I do remember Don the Beachcomber's Shack – but little more except the beauty of the ocean and beaches, palm trees, hibiscus flowers and great sunsets! Aloha you 'all!

CHAPTER 18

First Cruise to Asia

My first cruise to Asia was most exciting. I had joined the navy to see the world, and I could not think of anything more exciting than visiting many of the island groupings and to see and witness for the first time a culture I had read about and longed to visit but never thought I would see.

I had been aboard ship for about three or four months when we received our orders to set sail for the Hawaiian Islands and points east. Traveling from Long Beach, California, to Honolulu took approximately five days. The weather was terrific, and the dolphins were playing off both sides of our ship. The speed of our ship was a lazy twenty knots an hour. Life was beautiful. My duty was outside, up in the superstructure. Boy, was I glad I had joined the navy!

On the fifth day, we were steaming past Pearl Harbor. Suddenly it dawned on me that, just a few short years earlier, the Japanese had suddenly and without warning attacked the island from different directions, wave after wave, with bombs, torpedoes, and other destructive weapons in the process of destroying our naval fleet. It was a somber moment and a time of serious reflection. I tried to picture Battleship Row and perhaps where the Arizona was berthed, as well as the many ships that were destroyed or damaged. I remember the emotions I felt as we cruised past this historic harbor.

But my emotions changed dramatically when we pulled into one of the city piers and moored. We could hear the music coming from the ukuleles, and as we got closer, we could see the hula dancers in their grass skirts, with their hips flowing gently to the sounds of the ukes. I had dreamed of this place, never knowing I would one day be there to see it. My emotions stirred my soul. *Am I actually here?* The palm trees were gently swaying in the breeze, and the flowers painted the landscape with so many beautiful colors. For just a moment, I thought I had died and my body had been transported to this island heaven.

In a few short hours, it was announced that liberty would begin at 5:00 p.m., and we should report back no later than midnight. We had changed our uniforms from dungarees to undress whites.

When liberty was announced, men were dressed and ready, waiting for the officer of the deck to open the gangplank. Men began crowding their way down to the pier to set foot on soil after five days at sea. I cannot describe the feelings I had when I first set foot on Hawaiian soil. It was a far cry from Seagraves, Texas.

From where the ship docked, Waikiki Beach wasn't too far. I am not sure I had ever heard about it, but for sure, I would never forget it. At the time there were only two large hotels on Waikiki Beach. One was the Royal Hawaiian, and the other was the Sheraton Waikiki. I have gone back to Honolulu and the islands seventeen times since then, and the hotels are now numerous and immense. It looks as if everyone was as impressed as I was and has made the islands into a vacation paradise. It has been and will always be my favorite retreat.

After a few days, we sailed out of the harbor for nine more days of blue water sailing, heading for Yokosuka, Japan. Upon our arrival, after having lived through World War II and seeing the Hawaiian Islands in all their splendor, Yokosuka seemed a thousand years behind Honolulu.

It was a city mired in ancient buildings and primitive transportation. The gift shops were filled with cheap souvenirs. I suspect it was much like it was before the war.

We would often travel by train to Yokohama or Tokyo to experience larger and more developed cities. In Yokosuka, the transportation was usually provided by pedicabs, which consisted of a bicycle hooked to what looked like a rickshaw. In the larger cities you would see pedicabs and taxis often fueled by charcoal.

Yokohama had more to offer the servicemen on liberty than the smaller towns, with better restaurants, clubs, and transportation.

We must have stayed in Japan for three months or so, touring the country, forming small squadrons of armed sailors, and marching up and down the streets with, of all things, wooden pieces as decoys for guns as a show of military occupation.

General MacArthur, who had his office in Tokyo, was the supreme commander of all Allied Forces in the Far East. Both morning and evening, Japanese people would line the streets and bow to him when he went by. Wooden pieces and a conquering hero—something was quite artificial somewhere.

While we were in Japan, we circled all three islands that make up the country, visited most of the major cities, and often paraded through the towns as a reminder of the US occupation of a defeated country. I am sure it was humiliating for a proud people defeated in war. There was a look of disdain on their faces as we marched proudly by, reminding them of a bitter defeat.

We also visited the devastated cities of Hiroshima and Nagasaki, ghost shrines to a nuclear war. Theirs was a once-proud people humbled by the might of thunderous and fiery explosions. I walked the grounds of both cities, where there was not a twig of greenery four years after the drop. I saw cartons of soft drinks with all of the bottles were melted together without shape. As far as the eye could see in any direction, there was no sign of new growth, and large steel beams were twisted like pretzels. There was no sound, simply silence, where people once trod and traffic was congested—a silent reminder that war is extremely devastating. What I saw was a picture of utter destruction where at one time people and industry were evidence of God's presence. I shall never ever forget it! May the grace of God Almighty never allow it again.

CHAPTER 19

Hong Kong

With great memories and a multitude of questions we left Japan with feelings of uncertainty. What were the true feelings experienced? Were the Japanese people humbled beyond expression or were they masking their feelings? How can one go from being the conqueror to being the conquered? Was there a deep humility that accompanied defeat or was there a masked distain for those who crossed their shores? I could not read the faces of those with whom I came into contact they were expressionless. The language barrier made it difficult to communicate or evaluate with any sense of reality. Perhaps another day!

We headed southward from Japan and passed within sight of Okinawa, where one of the toughest and bloodiest battles was fought before the invasion of Japan proper. It stirred within me the remembrance that one of our neighbors' sons had been killed on Okinawa. It was a sad day for the whole community when the telegram came: "I regret to inform you that your son, Ira Joe Allen, has been killed in combat." All of this occurred not too long after another telegram had come to another farmhouse less than one mile away: "We regret to inform you that Raymond McDaniel has been killed on Iwo Jima." The scars of war run deep and wide.

We were sailing southerly with no inclination of what was going on or about to happen. But the further South we sailed; the seas were beginning to grow rougher. The command of our ship was slow to inform us that we were moving into the path of a typhoon. A huge tropical depression was forming as we continued toward Hong Kong.

I had never been in a typhoon before, but I understood that we were in the season for heavy seas. The weather leaving San Francisco was always a little rough because of ground swells beneath the surface of the ocean. This type of weather generally produces seasickness. Many of our crew was looking a little pale.

The farther we traveled the rougher the seas. We were given a little education about the storm and what to expect. One of the first things to do is to batten down the hatch's topside. Everything must be secured to keep loose objects from being claimed by the Mother of the deep. All personnel are taken below deck. No man overboard in this weather. The bridge which is perhaps three or four levels above the deck and is the Captain's Command Center.

Each typhoon has basically four quadrants with each quadrant a little more severe as one moves around a clockwise system. Each ensuing quadrant is more severe than the one before. The goal of the Navigator is to keep the vessel in a less dangerous quadrant. Beware! There are no quadrants free of the storm.

Within hours we were tossing and rolling and pitching. One could go up into the superstructure and get a clear view of the churning sea and ship being tossed unmercifully around. Sea sickness was rampant. Even though our ship was of enormou8s size it was being tossed about like a huge toy. The bow would sink beneath the huge waves and water would wash over the top of the masts. The ship would roll from side to side, groaning and moaning something awful.

Smaller ships accompanying us would seem to ride the waves high and be several feet higher than we were and in the next instant we would be seemingly along among heavy waves. These were the times one longed to be among the flat sand hills of West Texas. Only the mighty engines of our ship and the skill of the Navigator would prevent us from being drawn into a more dangerous quadrant.

We rode this storm for what seemed an eternity with the moaning and groaning of man and vessel until we found quieter areas. Within a few days we could see the harbor entrance into Hong Kong. When we finally moored, we were surrounded by junkies and sampans, hundreds of native fishing crafts manned by the typical Chinese fisherman with his large round hat that covered his head.

Once we were securely berthed, liberty was sounded for "Port and Starboard" liberty, which meant you were permitted to go ashore every other day. Luckily, I had liberty the first day. You could hire a "rickshaw" for perhaps a quarter which most could hold only one passenger. So, there was a string of rickshaws pulling sailors (Generals on a run) to the downtown area. To the best of my knowledge there was only one large hotel in the downtown area, while there were many small hotels adjacent to downtown and out in the suburbs.

What I learned was that the island of Kowloon, in the harbor, was off limits to enlisted men, so I am sure it catered to officers and more refined clientele.

When we arrived at Hong Kong and received our first liberty, several of us went to a restaurant in the Hong Kong Hotel for what we thought would be a lavish dinner. But being ignorant of the menu and Chinese food, each one of us, after a brief conversation, decided to stick with the tried and true—we ordered a steak with six fried eggs. Never have I eaten a meal that tasted so good. (What the meat was, though, I have no idea.)

I found Hong Kong to be a fascinating city. Since we were ignorant of Chinese history and culture, we hardly knew what to do or where to go except for doing sailor things, about which I will not go into detail.

The architecture I noticed was mainly of the European or British variety in the business district, but in the residential areas it was a mixture of stucco apartments or wood with bamboo interiors. I really do not remember much about anything else. I do remember the fishing boats (the jargon for them was "junks"). The outlying islands, which were plentiful, were all off-limits to enlisted men. I supposed they housed the more affluent population and officer's quarters. We were there only five or six days, and then we hit the ocean again for even more adventures.

CHAPTER 20

The Philippine Islands

Our next port would be in the Philippine Islands. I have often said that "I spent a year in the Philippines, one winter." When one sails in toward Manila Bay the trip takes you between the islands of Bataan and Corregidor. I remember the day very well, it was November 24, 1949, my sister's birthday. We would, in fact, celebrate Thanksgiving Day with a special Thanksgiving lunch with all the trimmings.

For the time entering, I was alone sitting on my Director's platform (Battle Station) while contemplating what happened in 1942 as the Japanese perpetrated on the American servicemen the infamous Death March. Even though alone, I was very somber remembering the cruelty of the event by the Japanese soldiers. The Americans were grossly under armed and unprepared while they were over run. The memory of the Death March became sort of the battle cry in the Pacific Theater. I remember my brother who spent 30 months in the Pacific going from island to island recapturing the ground that was lost.

We sailed past Subic Bay, where the United States maintained a significant Naval Base, into Manila Bay. We anchored out on the Southeast side of the bay near a little village town Cavite City. Cavite City, by any stretch of the imagination, was not a suitable "liberty" port. The town was small, dirty and with inadequate facilities of any kind to serve the U.S.S. Helena. We managed the situation for three months, but it could have been disastrous.

On one occasion we left Cavite City and went South to the Island of Panay on a Goodwill call. Once moored in a very small village, the Mayor of the Township paid a welcome visit to our Captain or Admiral.

He was dressed, I am assuming in his best formal wear, (of typical dress for that region) pants about four inches above his ankles, no shoes or socks and wearing a "straw sailors" hat. I am sure he was given the dignity if his office.

A friend of mine and I were granted leave for a couple of hours and we walked through the village of Floilo, where there were a few small houses scattered around, with pigs roaming the streets. We saw no merchants or people to visit with. We stayed ashore for a couple of hours, gave up our quest and returned to the ship. Perhaps it was a welcome visit but nothing Washington would be interested in knowing. Back to Cavite City. The most I can say about our visit has already been said.

We left the Philippines cruising near several of the island groups mentioned during the war. When we arrived back near Iwo Jima, we were anchored out and the "Flag" was transferred to another heavy cruiser. I believe the U.S.S. Toledo, and then we made a stop in Hawaii and then back to Long Beach.

This was a long and interesting cruise, aimed at perhaps easing some tensions with Japan and the rest good will to all!

CHAPTER 21

A Taste of War

On June 25, 1950, the North Koreans invaded South Korea as an act of aggression. The invasion, as I understand, was totally surprising and tremendously devastating. No doubt there was a desperate appeal for military support. I was never told exactly how we became involved, but here is my story from the beginning.

I was serving aboard the *USS Helena* (CA-75) moored in our home port of Long Beach, California. We had just returned from a lengthy tour of Asia, and our command had established three consecutive leave parties, allowing the crew to visit their homes for a specific time frame. Leave party number one had gone and returned, and the second leave party was on their time away at the beginning of the conflict. I had signed up for the third leave party but was unable to take advantage of it because the second leave party was recalled, and we began to make preparations for another trip abroad, this time for combat. I do not remember exactly how I felt, but we were caught up with an uneasy feeling because most of us had never seen action.

After all the preparations had been made, such as taking on rations and ammunition and whatever we needed to face the enemy, we worked diligently to see that our ship was in the finest condition possible for what may lay ahead. We were given orders around the first or second week of July to get underway to meet other vessels of all types somewhere east of California, combining Cruiser Division Three with perhaps one hundred other ships to form a task force heading toward Korea.

We had been at sea for several days when our command decided to stage a man-overboard drill. This drill was always conducted in the same manner. One of our crew had constructed a dummy, known as Oscar, from the material that was stuffed into our life jackets to ensure its floatation. When the signal came, someone would throw old Oscar over the side while someone else would yell, "Man overboard, port!" or "starboard," as the case may be. The ship would turn in the needed direction to keep the ship's propellers from hitting Oscar. A lifeboat with crew would be lowered into the water, and the boat would *putt-putt* out to the spot where Oscar was floating, rescue him, and return to the ship to be hoisted back to the deck, where Oscar would be given immediate attention.

Thus, begins the most horrible personal story of my navy career. During this particular devastating event, I was assigned to be the JV phone-talker on the bridge, where the ship's command was stationed. My phone was connected to perhaps three or four other duty stations, including the lifeboat station involving the rescue of Oscar. When the dummy was thrown over the side, the familiar shout was heard: "Man overboard, starboard!" Immediately our ship turned starboard, as did every ship in the task force, synchronized by Central Command.

The lifeboat station said in their phone, "Bridge, Lifeboat! Request permission to lower the boat!"

I said, "Bridge to Lifeboat, I have had no word from the officer of the day!"

Repeatedly, the lifeboat phone talker said, "Bridge, request permission to lower the boat."

"Lifeboat, wait a minute," I replied. "I have had no word."

Again, two or three times, he made the same request.

Finally, I said, "Lower the boat!"

Immediately, our ship's captain stormed onto the bridge and shouted, "Who ordered the lifeboat to be lowered?" My heart leaped to my throat! (I had created the most lethal situation in my whole life!) Someone broke military law, oh no, it was me. I ordered the lifeboat to be launched when only the ship's captain has the authority to do so. I could have soiled my dungarees but didn't. I did not say a single word. I knew that my name, rank, and everything else had gone down the tube. I waited for the next salvo. The officer of the day summoned me and said, "Call down to the lifeboat crew and ask who ordered that lifeboat to be lowered."

My goose was cooked! What could I do? Trembling to the bottom of my feet, I said into the phone, "Lifeboat, who ordered that boat to be lowered?" To my utter surprise, upon hearing what he said, I responded to him in a stern voice, "What do you mean, you don't know?"

Thinking I was an officer, he said, "Sir, I do not know!" With that, I felt a slight reprieve. I reported what he had told me to my superior. Everyone on the bridge was in absolute turmoil. What was going on? I was a wreck! I had given an order that I had no authority to give. No one else knew—and at that moment, I was not about to tell.

I felt terrible. I said to myself, "Pete, surely you are not that stupid!" But I had been. What should I do? Confess and take the punishment? What would they do to me if I did? Who would be the fall guy if I didn't? The lifeboat phone talker? My head was spinning. I was out of control. I decided to lay behind a log for a while and see what happened. To my amazement, nothing did!

When my duty was over, I went to my compartment, silent as a lamb. I did not dare to tell even my closest friend. I waited and waited for several days, but nothing ever happened. What would I have done had someone else been court-martialed? I really don't know. I would like to think I would have spoken up and taken the punishment, but I am not sure. My conscience troubled me for years. Who would I tell? What would happen two, five, or ten years later?

It seemed better to forget the incident and let sleeping dogs lie. But what if someone else was punished for what I did and kept silent? What if my parishioners found out? I like to think that, under fear someone else would be punished, I would have confessed. It sounds good.

This incident taught me a great lesson. Be honest. Confess and take the punishment. Don't let someone else suffer the punishment you should have suffered. As it was, no one suffered because of my stupidity, but I resolved never to repeat the same crime.

Once that incident was over, it was back to the war. I figured it would be a cinch compared to not following the correct procedure. The navy is great, but the penalties can be severe. But as long as one follows protocol, everything flows smoothly.

The task force arrived in Pearl Harbor five days after leaving Long Beach. After two or three days of refueling and taking on stores and ammunition, we set sail for Japan with our destination being Sasebo, where there was a fairly large harbor capable of handling a large fleet with fuel, stores, and an ammunition depot for us to come in occasionally to restock our supplies, as well as to provide two or three liberty opportunities, port and starboard, for the crews. Liberty was usually crowded and rowdy. If you keep a sailor at sea for thirty days at a time, where there are no women or booze, he tends to develop a wild side. The shore patrol officers were plentiful and busy.

Upon arrival in Korean waters, we met our sister ship, and the flag was transferred to our ship, placing us in command of the entire fleet on the East Coast of Korea. I am not sure if our jurisdiction extended farther than that or not.

As far as I experienced, our primary responsibility was patrolling the east coast of the northern part of the Korean Peninsula. We were regularly involved in destroying shore batteries up and down the coast, as well as destroying dangerous mines that had been dumped into the ocean by the train loads. Mines would break loose from the pack and float out to sea, risking damage to the fleet of ships up and down the coastal region. Our ship had a crew of US Marines on the bow equipped with M-1 rifles, whose sole duty was to blow up the mines. Our ship, being the flagship, usually had a minesweeper off our bow to run interference for us, but several of the ships that were directly exposed were damaged, often with several casualties.

Our ship never hit a mine, but we were hit a few times by the shore batteries; we had no casualties, but a few were injured. The shore batteries were usually very deceptive. In one instance, the North Koreans had perhaps a five-inch gun mounted on a railcar within a cave. They would bring the mounted gun to the front of the cave, fire it, and then immediately roll the rail car to the back of the cave where it was impossible for us to knock it out due to the trajectory of our shells. One day after we were struck by a shell and unable to effectively return their fire, we sent a call out to Japan for the air force to send some of their F-80 dive bombers. These planes would circle above the gun locations, and when the railcar would come out to the mouth of the cave, the F-80 would dive and drop an incendiary bomb in the cave, thus effectively destroying the gun placement.

This sort of warfare would continue for about a thirty-day period, we would proceed to Sasebo for refueling and replenishing, and then we would go back out to the same duty. There were times when we were forced to rescue troops who had been backed into a small peninsula. We would cover them while landing crafts went in to rescue them, and we would take them farther down on the main peninsula and let them fight their way back up to where they had been.

Special Mission

On one occasion, our ship was chosen for a special mission. The reason was unknown to me. We left the other ships and headed north beyond the border of North Korea adjacent to Manchuria.

We traveled northward with excessive speed until we reached a region just south of the Vladivostok River that cut between Russia and Manchuria. We could see some kind of a facility, but we could not determine what it was. It must have been very valuable to the war efforts of North Korea because, suddenly, perhaps twenty or more B-29s appeared and unloaded dozens of bombs on the facility, flattening it completely. I was impressed with the mission although I did not know exactly why the facility was being destroyed.

Immediately, we reversed our course and proceeded directly back to where we had been at practically flank speed. Mission accomplished— but what was it?

I have discovered that it is difficult to write about war without sounding too morbid or too heroic. I am a normal person with normal emotions, and when danger lurks, it is normal to be afraid. I have learned that the level of fear corresponds to the level of danger. If one does not properly know the level of danger, the level of fear may rise above the normal. The unknown generally raises emotions within us to an abnormal degree. To be blatantly honest, not to know the extent of the danger is to fear it abnormally.

On one occasion, we were ordered to the Taiwan Strait to stop a possible invasion of the Nationalist forces against the Communists. No action was required.

After several months, we were ordered home for a period of rest and recuperation.

CHAPTER 22

The Spruce Goose

One of the added attractions to having Long Beach, California as our home port, was the fact that Los Angeles harbor was also the temporary home of the "Spruce Goose", the name given the largest wooden airplane ever built. The formal name given the magnificent plane was the Hughes H-4 Hercules.

The reason for this plane being built was largely because the German submarines were decimating our cargo ships which were carrying valuable war material and troops to Europe. The plane was a brilliant idea whose time had passed.

The "Spruce Goose" was a sea plane which made only one flight, dating back to 1947, approximately one year before I saw her outside her hanger, dead in the water. What a beautifully constructed plane fabricated mainly out of birch, with some of the construction made of spruce. Perhaps the alliteration of Spruce-Goose caught one's attention more quickly.

The wingspan of the "Spruce Goose" was 320 feet. The plane was powered by eight engines. The United States government invested $18,000,000 in the aircraft, and Howard Hughes invested $7,000,000 of his own money. It is a magnificent looking aircraft, and I delighted to see it when we were leaving or entering the harbor. The "Spruce Goose" had a crew assigned to her as long as she was hangered in Long Beach.

The maiden flight occurred on November 2, 1947. The plane was only in the air less than thirty minutes although it had a range of 2983 miles.

CHAPTER 23

Prelude to Ministry

In 1951, I was serving in the US Navy aboard the cruiser *USS Helena* off the east coast of North Korea. We were near Wonsan Harbor and attempting to eliminate the shore batteries up and down North Korea as well as to destroy mines the North Koreans had generously dumped into the waters surrounding their country.

For some time, we had been anticipating that we would soon be relieved, which would allow us to return to the States. So we were making plans for our return home.

I was a member of a committee that decided to do something special for a handicapped child in the United States. We had run our plans by the ship's authority and had been given full approval to proceed. Our gift campaign went exceedingly well. We left no stone unturned, contacting every officer and enlisted man for a contribution. After about two weeks of constant fund-raising, we had acquired the amazing amount of sixty-five hundred dollars. That was a lot of money from a group of sailors, especially in 1951.

Upon full discussion of which city to pick for our fund-raiser, I recommended Helena, Montana, because our ship was named after that capital. Therefore, we wrote the chamber of commerce in Helena and asked it to send us several profiles of young children who qualified as candidates for our gift. Our request was airlifted, along with the ship's mail, to Japan, where the mail was transferred to the desired destinations.

Upon receiving our orders, we were to proceed to Sasebo, Japan, to prepare for our journey homeward. By the time we had made all the preparations, we received our response from the chamber in Helena. It had sent us eight or ten profiles.

We then set sail from Sasebo to Pearl Harbor in the Hawaiian Islands. The trip usually took about nine days, traveling at about twenty knots per hour. Nine days later, we arrived there and dispatched a committee member to fly to Helena to bring the young recipient and his foster parents to Long Beach, California, to greet our ship in about five days.

Much to our surprise, awaiting our arrival in Hawaii was the governor of Montana along with the mayor of Helena and other Montana dignitaries. All embarked our ship and sailed with us to Long Beach. It was a time to become acquainted with our honored guests and to celebrate what we had accomplished in our desire to serve a worthy candidate.

When we arrived in Long Beach, a pilot vessel met us in the outer harbor to escort us to our berth at one of the city piers. As we moved toward our berth, we were again surprised, this time seeing a monstrous crowd of nearly twenty-five thousand people cheering us home and standing on the piers and tops of buildings. We could not believe it!

As we moved into our berth, we were utterly astounded when a crew of national television reporters boarded our ship to the sound of a cheering audience. My heart rose to my throat when I remembered that I had been selected by my companions to offer the presentation speech before such an august body of people.

The young boy we had chosen was eight years of age. Dressed in his new cowboy suit adorned with a hat, pistols, boots, and a kerchief, he quickly took his place, accompanied by his foster parents and many honored guests, including the largest entourage of naval officers—of various ranks—I had ever seen. They quickly assembled in a grandstand that had been set up by the crew. My heart was pounding in my chest. This was the first speech I would ever give. I kept thinking, *Pete, keep your cool. Don't do anything stupid!* To stand before national television camera crews was not simply an honor but also the most frightening moment I had ever faced, except receiving enemy fire.

After what seemed like an eternity, I finished my remarks and knelt beside the boy, with the captain on the other side, and presented him the check that had been so generously donated by the officers and men of the *USS Helena.* I could not have been prouder or more honored.

Everything was a blur after that. I do not remember sitting down, the crowd dispersing, the many people I had met, saluting anyone, or anything else. Blank! The next thing I remember was being in my compartment and packing my seabag to begin my journey home for two weeks of leave. After about two hours, I went up to the deck, hoping the guests had left, because I did not want to see anyone. I was still a little hyper and a little unsure of how well I had performed.

As I descended the gangway, I noticed a couple standing on the pier. They had familiar faces. To my amazement, they were from my hometown in Texas and had moved to Santa Ana, California, some time ago. They had heard about our story and were there to welcome the hometown hero. I went home with them and spent the night there before I started the journey home the next day.

For many years, I wondered what had happened to this young boy. Hardly a month went by without my thinking about him in some way. The boy had become a part of me. Then, after sixty-two years, I decided to get in contact with him. I pulled up the white pages telephone directory for Helena, Montana, and found his name. One Sunday afternoon, I determined to call him. I dialed the phone, my heart pounding, and it rang several times. He would now be seventy years old, but I could still see him as a boy of eight. But there was no answer.

The next Sunday, I tried again. After three or four rings, a male voice answered the phone. I asked, "Is this Perry?"

The man said, "No, I am his son. Would you like to speak to my dad?"

I said that I would. In a short moment, another voice said, hello.

I said, "My name is Bryce Robertson. I do not know if you remember me, but I remember you. I am the man who handed you the check aboard the *Helena* many years ago."

He quickly said, "I remember you as if it were yesterday!"

I said, "I have always wondered what happened to you. Do you mind sharing with me something of your life?"

He began by telling me an extraordinary story. "My foster father was a banker. He took the check and invested it from the time I was eight years old until I graduated from high school. He said there was enough money in the fund to send me to college."

I responded with something like, "I am so glad that we were able to be a part of your education."

Then he said, "Mr. Robertson, you may not know that I became a minister."

"Well, you probably don't know that I also became a minister," I replied.

We exchanged our stories for a while, and then I said to him words that did not come from me but that formed in my mouth. "Perry, neither you nor I will ever know how God has worked His way in our lives. Perhaps it was through the gift we gave and you received."

These words have become indelible on my heart and mind. I genuinely believe that this was God's first call on my life!

And I thank God that this was not His last call on my life. In retrospect, sixty-two years later, I've seen how God can use us in ways beyond our anticipation and how He prepares us by our life experiences for the tasks He will ask us to perform.

My life, as set out in these pages, demonstrates how the Lord can use the commonest of clay to achieve His purposes.

SAILORS HELP HANDICAPPED BOY
Terry Wayne Ellis, 7, of Helena, Mont., who was born with a severe physical handicap, receives a check for $6,500 Saturday from FT3 Bryce C. Robertson, representing the crew of the cruiser Helena. The money was raised by the men of the Helena to aid deserving youngster "deprived of a proper start in life," as an expression of gratitude for their safe return from Korea waters. Civilians in the background are Mayor J. R. Kaiserman, left, of Helena and Gov. John W. Bonner of Montana. Capt. Lawrence H. Martin of the Helena sits between them.

(This photo was from the presentation of the gift to the young boy in 1952) It came from the ceremony proper and was in the cruise book and public newspapers. I possess an 8 1/2" x 11" print of the same picture. Should be clear to use. Boy is deceased

CHAPTER 24

Early Years of Marriage

I am not exactly sure of how and when I first met the woman who later became my wife. I had known members of her extended family for several years before we met. My wife, Eppie June Freeman, was reared on a small ranch near Quemado, New Mexico. She would make occasional visits to Seagraves, Texas, my hometown, to visit her relatives, although I never had the opportunity to formally meet her until several years later.

She attended a rural school for a while with some of her kinsfolk several miles from Seagraves. It was a rather strange coincidence that one of her sisters, Bobbie, lived in Seagraves and dated one of my brothers, and when he enlisted in the military, they married before he shipped out to Watton, England, with the Eighth Air Force. Bobbie and I became great friends several years before Eppie and I met.

Our first real encounter came when I was home on leave from the navy and stopped off at Hurley, New Mexico, to visit with my brother and sister-in-law, and Eppie was there. The next time we met was in Dallas when I again came home on leave and my brother and his wife were also in Dallas visiting my parents. Eppie and I went on a couple of dates while I was home and again when I visited them in New Mexico on my return to California. A few sparks flew between us, yet I never felt the romance held real promise.

Boy, was I wrong! It is all still a swirl! It happened so fast that I still can't fully explain it. But the first thing I knew, she was on a bus heading to the Arizona–California state line, and a navy friend of mine and his wife were driving me to meet her at a bus station in a place named Salome, Arizona. We arrived there around one o'clock in the morning of January 12, 1952, and found a justice of the peace shortly thereafter. We woke him up and procured our marriage license, and then he performed our ceremony. We were quickly on our way back to Long Beach, California—as husband and wife! I was twenty-one, and Eppie was eighteen. If this happened any way other than I have explained it, you tell me!

I had to report to my ship by 8:00 a.m. the next day, so Eppie spent the day with Shirley Kinder, and when I received liberty that afternoon, I went to meet my bride. I frankly can't tell you the sequence of events for the next couple of days. But within a short time, Eppie had found us a small apartment to rent. I say it was small because I could stretch out my arms and touch both sides of the apartment at the same time. It was an elongated room, perhaps twenty to twenty-five feet long, with a sitting space, kitchen, dining room, and bedroom all in a row. It was cozy, but it was not my idea of what home was supposed to look like. But, at my navy pay grade, it was the only home I could afford.

We lived there for two or three months. I needed to be at sea for about a week, and when I returned, Les Hardesty, one of my shipmates, called his wife, and she said, "Is Pete with you?"

He said that I was, and Becky replied, "Tell Pete not to go home. He doesn't live there anymore!" While I was at sea, Eppie had rented a small (but not *that* small) apartment next door to Les and Becky Hardesty. This arrangement resulted in a long and fruitful friendship that outlasted Eppie's life and goes on even until today. I still get Christmas card from them postmarked "Eugene, Oregon."

We lived in that apartment until I was ready to be discharged from the navy. I was transferred to the Naval Departure Center in San Diego, California, to await my release. Eppie went by bus to Apache Junction, Arizona, to await my arrival within two weeks.

After we remained there with her folks for a few days, we boarded a bus bound for Plains, Texas, to visit one of my brothers and his family for a couple of days before they drove us on to Seagoville, Texas, to visit my parents.

Before we arrived in West Texas, my brother had brokered a job for me with Shell Oil Company in Denver City, Texas. Only a few days after we had driven to Seagoville, Shell called and advised that they wanted me to report to work within a few short days.

We returned to West Texas, and as requested I reported to work in my first civilian job after being discharged from the navy. I was excited about having a job with a regular income, and I was quasi-excited about becoming a welder. Although I was basically pleased with the company, I felt uneasy about where I was placed and the level of security and promise the position offered me. My interests seemed to point in a different direction. I felt that I was more interested in a career than a job.

But obviously it was going to take more time for me to figure out my future. In the meantime, I needed to hang onto the job.

When I was discharged from the navy with a new wife, my priorities changed. When Eppie and I moved to Plains, the first thing we did was to get established in a church. Although we were inexperienced, our hearts were leading us in new directions. The pastor of the Methodist church quickly asked me to teach a young person's Sunday school class.

I said that I would and immediately felt spiritually confirmed. How do I know that? Because I did!

Regardless of how I felt about my new job, I felt better about myself. Career employment took on lesser importance, but growth in the Spirit leaped in gigantic proportion.

Gradually, I felt that I was turning a corner. Employment was a way to pay my bills, but accepting greater spiritual responsibility was a way to honor God and live my life.

CHAPTER 25

Admiral for a Day

The year was 1950, I was serving a four-year hitch in the U.S. Navy, aboard the U.S.S. Helena (CA-75) moored in Long Beach, California. After our extensive tour of the Far East including Japan, Hong Kong with a three month visit to the Philippine Islands, along with a couple of stops at different Island groupings before returning home – a long exhausting tour but tremendously rewarding.

After arriving back in Long Beach, I was granted a ten day leave to go home to Texas to see my parents and a girlfriend I had dated on the last leave home and whom I had written a few times.

After returning to California my girlfriend and I decided to get married and she boarded a bus and met me in a most unusual place at the border of California and Arizona, by the name of Salome, Where She Danced, Arizona.

A Navy friend and his wife drove me to meet my new bride to be arriving at 1:00am the next morning. Arizona permitted marriages at any hour of any day. So, my young bride of 18 years and I, along with our companions, knocked on the door of a Justice of the Peace around 1:30am, where we were quickly wed and back on our way to Long Beach before 2:00am. The J.P. wheezed a bit (I am sure from the coal mountain air) but legally was able to tie the knot.

We were safely back in Long Beach before breakfast. Our hosts fed us cereal and toast and we slept a couple of hours, Eppie on the couch and me in one of their living room chairs. Both my navy friend and I reported to the ship by the proper time and we both applied for a 48-hour pass for my new wife and I to find a place we could afford to rent.

So early the next morning we began our search for our first "home". It really wasn't too difficult for us to find a place to lodge. At my pay grade – we looked cheap!

Within three or four visits we found it! A lovely furnished garage apartment, replete with kitchen, living, dining, bedroom and bath, all one area from front to back! The apartment contained everything we needed from sitting space to dining (including kitchen) bedroom and bath, all neatly arranged in a space about 26' long and about 9' wide. Don't try to explain how we managed this for two months before finding another place, because I would have told you, if I was able, - but never discovered the secret!

During the first month of our marriage a marvelous opportunity became mine. There was a very popular television show airing, at the time, in the Hollywood TV Studios by the name of "Queen for a Day!"

Hollywood sent an invitation to our ship for two busloads of sailors to come to Hollywood and attend a "spin-off" of Queen for a Day by the gripping title of, Admiral for a Day! My friend Les (a buddy and a neighbor) and I were chosen to attend this TV spectacular, so we boarded the bus and made our way down Rodeo Drive to the heart of television Hollywood.

Once seated in the large auditorium, an announcer began to call out ticket numbers on tickets we had been issued on our way into the theater. After two or three names had been called, the name of my friend Lester Hardesty was announced, and he excitedly ran to the stage. Behold, after a couple of numbers were called my name was spat out over the PA system and I proudly joined my friend Les on the stage.

I am not sure how many contestants were included but I think as many as a dozen! Once we were on the stage and the clock struck the hour – out came the leader of the program, Jack Bailey himself, to begin the contest of who would be crowned as Admiral of the Day!

Bailey interviewed the object of the show and gradually introduced the contestants. All of this was amid the glamour and glitter of National Television with Mr. Bailey performing in all his glory. It was truly exciting.

After endless commercials Bailey began interviewing each contestant. No doubt he had read all the papers written by the contestants on what they wanted if they were selected "Admiral of the Day!"

I had written my article as a newly married person who needed everything! To know how the contest came out, I would have done something radically different. (with my acquired ingenuity I may have walked away with Hollywood proper).

So, when Jack Bailey approached the contestant who later won, he quizzed him a remarkable and comical way on him wanting a "Coon-dog!" The young man was from Kentucky and lived on a farm and had always wanted a "Coon-dog".

I have thought about this program over the years. IT was a great request! It brought the house down! Bailey only had to be himself – the request easily won him the prize. My paper was too normal, to expected from a newlywed. Wanting a coon-dog was phenomenal! It was precious! (I will never know if coon-dog was his idea or Bailey's!) but I will give credit to the young man coming up with a brilliant idea.

CHAPTER 26

From Heavy Cruiser to Oil Refinery

Eppie and I rented a garage apartment until we could try to find some better housing. One of the first orders of business was to purchase an automobile. The nearest automobile dealer was in Brownfield, Texas, some twenty-five miles away. My brother took me there, and I found a fairly clean 1946 Chevrolet. I arranged a loan with an installment plan and drove away in the first automobile I had owned since I had joined the navy.

The next Monday I arrived at my new job, excited about learning how to weld with both arc and gas. Little did I know that it would be months before I could use anything but a cutting torch. Welding is an art, and one does not learn an art in a week.

Oil was big business in West Texas, as well as in other regions. Oil was discovered around Denver City in the late 1930s and early 1940s. Many cotton farmers went from rags to riches literally overnight.

I am not talking about light duty here because welding was hard and the hours were long. I did not have to be rocked to sleep every night. The dangers were ever present. We were constantly around high octane fuel. Any spark in the wrong place could set off an explosion.

Every day was different in the workplace, but at lunchtime it was routine. Everyone brought his own lunch, and the rush was on to get to the dining area and start our daily domino game while we ate. The competition in dominos was fierce, and the meals were routine. There was nothing to brag about in the lunch pail but much to brag about after the games.

But when the whistle blew, it was back to work. One day the competition was so fierce in dominos that one person completely forgot to eat his lunch. The friendships made there have lasted forever. I still think of the crew every once in a while although it has been well over sixty years, with much water under the bridge.

Over all, Shell is a fine company with good benefits. But, in reality, I was not looking for simply employment; I was looking for a life.

CHAPTER 27

When My Life Began to Change

One of my older brothers and his family lived in the same town where Eppie and I did, the same county where I had been raised, and it was delightful to be near them. He was the one brother I related to the most when I was growing up.

Because of my upbringing, I felt a strong need to relate to my parents' church, although my brother was disappointed that I did not attend the church of his choice. The first Sunday after we had settled in, we visited the First Methodist Church in Plains.

The pastor, Reverend Finis Pickens, an older gentleman, greeted us with warmth and genuine hospitality. He was not the finest preacher I had ever heard, but he was the sweetest man I could ever find to nurture me in my faith journey.

My wife and I had decided to join the church on a profession of faith and to be open to whatever God had in store for us. I was tremendously excited to take this step toward becoming a disciple of the Lord Jesus Christ even though I was ignorant of what it was going to take and perhaps a little reluctant to fully commit myself. This was a major step for me, but I was not quite ready to commit myself fully. God's grace was at work in me, but it took a few years for it to come to fruition.

Within two or three weeks, I was asked to teach a children's class. I readily agreed and began to read and study the material, ignorant though I was. I could not remember ever opening the Bible seriously and trying to understand the will of God for my life, much less for the lives of the young people under my tutelage. I was a little uncomfortable at first for I needed to experience it before I could understand how to teach it. I am sure I was totally inadequate, but the children tolerated me decently.

The class experience went on for several months before I was asked to take other leadership roles in the church. The church was filled with senior adults, and I am sure they welcomed fresh blood. The church grew in its importance to me. The pastor was giving me more credit than I deserved. I enjoyed the attention he gave me, but I felt that I was not growing in the faith as I had envisioned.

An issue arose at my workstation with Shell. I was working with a hardened group of oil company employees who were not on the same page with me. The language was undesirable, and the employee work standards were below what I expected. I discovered that I had begun to emulate them instead of practicing my new spiritual experience. I felt uncomfortable, yet I relented too many times. This was troubling for me. How could I maintain my faith in an atmosphere of frivolity? This has been an age-old problem with the yearnings of people of faith and people who are not interested at all or who ridicule others for their position. Shell Oil began to become worrisome for me, but for the time I could not even think about leaving the company. To give up a salary for the unknown takes a lot of thought, courage, and a full measure of hope. It is a "God thing" to go from something to nothing. But God has never failed me! When we learn to trust Him in all things, we can live a secure and fulfilled life. To me, this was the beginning of Easter!

CHAPTER 28

Decision Time Cometh

Life does not wait for a person who is misplaced. Since my youth, I have had the dream of acquiring a college education. But my dream never seemed to come to fruition.

> When I was discharged from the navy, I banked my hopes on the fact that I could possibly attend under the GI Bill. But time got away from me, and I was facing a critical deadline. My discharge papers said that I must be enrolled in a college or university before May 28, 1955. The problem was that I could find no college that started that early. Also, I had received the sad news that my mother's cancer was beginning to accelerate, and she had perhaps only six months to live. So I decided to sell my home in Plains, leave Shell, move to Dallas, and attend the American Barber College. Afterward, I could work with my brothers and be near my mother. It was a risk, but I really needed to be near my mother during her last days. School was important, but being near my mother was a necessity.

A college education was a pipe dream now that reality had set in. My home sold quickly, with a handsome profit. I encouraged my father to build me another home in Seagoville, just around the corner from where my parents lived.

I searched the nearby colleges and universities but found none that began before or on May 28, 1955. I had two brothers who were barbers, so I enrolled in the American Barber College in Dallas to acquire my license. After six months, I graduated from the college and joined my brothers in a three-chair shop aptly named Robertson Brothers Barber Shop.

For several months, being with my brothers was rewarding. They were both journeyman barbers, while I was yet an apprentice. But after a while the glamour wore off, and I once again felt that I were misplaced vocationally. If the truth be known, a barber demonstrates his or her skills in order to earn the almighty dollar, not necessarily to impress his fellow workers but to put the grub on the table.

The barber business is spotty during the week but excessively busy on Saturdays. My brothers and I would play a lot of checkers during business hours during the week, but on Saturdays, we might not sit down for twelve hours running. That is grueling work!

Needless to say, for someone who is often preoccupied with a call to ministry or wanting to be engaged in a college or a university curriculum, working in a barber shop can make one become terribly distracted and despondent.

The first Sunday after our move to Seagoville, Eppie and I united with the local Methodist Church, and I was immediately recruited to work with the youth fellowship that very evening. All of this went well, and I was excited.

I attended church regularly and became involved in a leadership capacity within the youth department and within the inner workings of the church itself.

My situation simply began to grow worse. I became disenchanted with the barber trade, and my life was empty and unfulfilled. I spent more time with the minister than I did behind my barber chair.

Again, the urge to attend college raised its head. I began to experience more and more signs that perhaps God was calling me into ministry. I consulted with the pastor of my church, and he took seriously the vocational struggles I was going through. After about a year of inner struggle, I was convinced that I indeed was being called to enter the pastoral ministry. From there on, my path was clear. The struggle was gone

One Sunday morning, when the pastor gave the invitation to those who were being challenged to make any kind of decision, I walked down the aisle and met him at the altar. He asked me a simple question; "Why did you come?"

I responded, "Because above all else I want to become a minister of Jesus Christ!"

He then asked, "Do you have any reservations?"

I said, "No!" Yet, at the same time, I said to myself, Lord, I am about to take a leap, but You had better catch me! I did, and He did!

Suddenly, it happened. My precious mother died with her six sons and one daughter gathered around her bed. She was a woman of tremendous faith. She died attempting to sing "Amazing Grace."

My mother had always said that she wanted her six sons to be her pallbearers, and we were, with my sister walking slowly behind the casket. To our utter surprise, our father died of a heart attack three months later, on my mother's birthday.

Before I made the decision for ministry, my parents had both died; therefore I could not celebrate the moment with them. But they were there in spirit, and I knew they were well pleased. I was my mother's youngest, and I know she had great expectations for me.

With that commitment made, I began to work with the minister to enroll in the undergraduate program at Southern Methodist University—with no money but with a burning desire. But could I continue with the monetary arrangements? I had a partial scholarship but had to pay around $250.00 per semester out of pocket.

But with my decision to enter the ministry came the necessity to consider two things: one, where could I live that would make my travel to college or seminary relatively easy, and two, where could I perhaps find a staff job in a church that would enhance my calling and bring in a few shekels?

About that time, my current pastor, Bob Middlebrooks, shared with me that he was being considered for one of two pastorates. One was in Wichita Falls, and the other was probably First Methodist Church in Richardson. Richardson's population at that time was about nine thousand people, most of whom were east of Central Expressway.

Bob kept me informed, and I prayed fervently that it would be Richardson. It seemed that to have everything in one place would serve my needs perfectly. Richardson proved to be the place, and my move was scheduled for the first of June 1957.

Richardson became a dream come true. I was assigned some fundamental duties that grew in time, and I also found a job cutting hair in a shopping center on Saturdays. My wife and I rented one side of a duplex, and she continued working at the mailing room at SMU. School was stimulating, the church work was challenging, and life was good!

CHAPTER 29

American Barber College

In 1955 I was employed by Shell Oil Company in a refinery in Denver City, Texas. Due to my mother's illness and impending death, I left my job and we moved to Seagoville, Texas near where my parents lived. My wife and I lived with my parents until we could have a house built very near other members od my family. I had sold my home where we had lived so I had a little money on which we could live before I found another place of employment.

I wanted very much to begin a college degree program, but there was no summer school starting before my veteran's eligibility ran out. I had two brothers who were barbers, so they encouraged me to enroll in barber school on the G.I, bill, which I did, not because I saw myself as a career barber, but that it was best for me at the moment. The barber trade was something that I could do while preparing for something else.

So, I enrolled in the American Barber College, 606 Commerce St in Dallas, commuting five days a week, a round trip of approximately forty miles. I was mildly excited to being enrolled in barber school, knowing that I would always have a back-up trade where I could work full or part-time if and when I needed to do so.

The early days went something like this: I first had to purchase all my equipment. My brothers were very helpful. I purchased two different signature electric clippers, razor, comb and brushes, and items suggested by the school and my brothers.

My first day on the job I had no customers by designs. I spent the entire day learning how to make and keep my new razor sharp. Lesson

1: One is more apt to cut a customer with a dull razor than a sharp one, technique is a learned experience.

After becoming familiar with my tools, about the third day, I was introduced to my first customer. I was set up in a four-chair cubicle known as the "free department". Most of our customers were 'street people' who were asleep within a few minutes when they sat down in our chair. Therefore, there was no time limit for either a haircut or shave. Sometimes it would take an hour for a shave. If by chance, you have wounded someone with the razor there was plenty of time to begin over and over and over. The instructor spent very little time with you, generally at your request.

When the floor instructor thought you had progressed to a point, he would put you on the 'pay' floor and rotate chairs each day. The customers believed that the closer your chair was to the front, the more experienced you were…wrong! Haircuts were twenty-five cents, as also shaves. Poor customers!

It was surprising how many businesspersons visited the college. Convenience? Prudent? Most of these customers became regulars if they liked your work. The college received the payment for service. The students received no compensation except for an occasional gratuity. We were allowed to converse freely with our customers. The hours were 9 to 5.

Mixed in with our floor times, we also had to attend a one-hour class every day that pertained to barbering in every facet as well as learning the circulatory system and hair and scalp condition. I became4 a substitute teacher in the classroom, which provided me a small compensation.

When I graduated from barber school, I was offered a job as both floor instructor and textbook studies. This was short lived, due to the fact that two of my brothers and I leased a three-chair barber shop and started up our own business. With a likely name – Robertson Brothers Barber Shop. Both were journeyman barbers and I learned a great deal observing them in their work. I soon learned that compensation meant that you not only became faster, you also became more efficient.

I have thoughts every now and then, what if I had not gone to barber school? What other trade or occupation could have supported me as well as the barber trade has done? I have had instant supplemental work whenever I have needed it. My barbering helped me, as I worked part-time through S.M.U. What other trade could have helped me as much?

CHAPTER 30

The Beginning of a College Education

From sometime in my early life, I had dreamed of getting a college education. What at one time had been absolutely impossible became a dim hope and, finally, a reality. I always felt that I had the interest and ability to attend and graduate from a college or university. I never dreamed, however, it would be Southern Methodist University. (I have a habit of calling it Harvard of the South.)

I enrolled as a pre-theological student and was assigned to the vice-president's office for ten hours a week for two years. I attended the university until I graduated with a bachelor's of arts in social studies, being directed by the seminary to the proper courses I should take before I enrolled in Perkins School of Theology.

I am extremely grateful to Southern Methodist University for years of education, mainly on scholarship. Being a future student at the seminary, I was granted generous hours on scholarship. There is no way I can ever repay that except through my service to the church, which has now lasted sixty-two years. That translates to little revenue to the university but years in the name of the Methodist Church.

I graduated from Perkins in 1965 and was appointed as pastor of the First Methodist Church in Van Alstyne, Texas. It felt so good to have my education behind me, but I realized later that my real education was still before me. Academics is one thing, but experience is another. I do not think one can have either without having both. There is valuable education on both sides of the fence. At times, one side of the educational spectrum appears to have the upper hand, while at other times experience validates one's education.

I am proud to be an alumnus of Southern Methodist University. I would not take anything for the years I spent in the classrooms absorbing data from many fields. But I am even more proud to be an ordained United Methodist clergyman who has served many different appointments with no blemishes on my record, now in a retired capacity in good standing.

I now live in retirement thanking God for every day He has allowed me to serve. And I am grateful to Him for enabling me to serve with some distinction.

I owe Southern Methodist University more than my gratitude, but my financial status forbids a large gift. My service to the church is a poor substitute for the financial support I wish I could give to SMU, but my deepest appreciation will have to do until I discover the abandoned Superstition Gold Mine in Arizona.

CHAPTER 31

First Baby! Yes ... No ... Yes!

My wife and I had been married for about six years and desperately wanted to have a baby. After what seemed an eternity, our obstetrician informed us that a child was on the way. How thrilled we were! We read books, attended classes, consulted our doctor regularly, and waited impatiently for the grand entrance.

Finally, one morning around two o'clock, my wife awakened me and yelled, "It's time!" I said, "Are you sure?" She yelled back, "*Yes!*" So we loaded the car with everything imaginable and headed out for Baylor Hospital in Dallas—the Florence Nightingale Maternity Hospital, in particular.

I had made a few practice runs in both day and night, just to be sure. I was driving toward Baylor on Greenville Avenue at a generous speed, and when I turned right on Ross Avenue in front of what was then Sears Department Store, I saw a flashing red light in my rear view mirror.

I pulled over to the side, rather impatiently, and waited for a slow-walking, gum-chewing gumshoe to approach the car. The policeman had already pulled his ticket book from his pocket when he said, "You know that you were speeding?" I wanted to be funny and say, "Not as fast as I wanted!"

But he looked a bit impatient, so I leveled with him. "Officer, my wife is about to deliver a baby, and I am on the way to Baylor!" His expression turned ashen, and he blurted out in good police etiquette, "Follow me!" He spun his wheels getting around me, and I tried my best to stay up with him.

He turned into the emergency department of Florence Nightingale after radioing for assistance, and out came a crew of nurses, doctors, technicians, business office personnel—you name it. We were ushered directly to the delivery room. All of them disappeared into a private area and left me standing in the hallway.

About four and a half hours later, the doctor came out and said, "False alarm!" *What?* I handed my wife over to a group of people who sequestered her behind closed doors, telling me nothing; I got through an episode of *Dragnet*; and I waited for hours, anxiously waiting for the tiny cry of my newborn child, only to hear the doctor say, "False alarm"? Was my wife the victim of weight gain, or was she really pregnant?

The doctors attempted to be sympathetic. "The answers are, no, she is not the victim of weight gain; yes, she really is pregnant; but the truth is that she is not ready to deliver. So, what we are saying, Mr. Robertson, is take her home until she is ready."

So, we loaded the car, headed back up Greenville Avenue, and climbed the stairs to our garage apartment wondering if all of this was simply a joke. The signs indicated that it was no joke, but when would the baby come? You guessed it! At about two o'clock the next morning, I was awakened with the same words—softened, but just as sure: "It is time!" So, just as deliberately, we grabbed the bag, loaded the car, backed out more slowly, and headed up Greenville Avenue toward Baylor. I am sure I was driving the same speed I had been the previous day but with a cautious eye, watching out for "Jack Webb." What would I say if I got pulled over again? But there was no need to explain. I never saw him.

We made it to Baylor, and before long, Eppie was whisked into the delivery room. After several anxious minutes, the doctor came out with the joyful announcement: "It's a boy! Nine pounds, and (I believe) thirteen ounces." Thank God, all was well and healthy! We named him Stephen Andrew Robertson. His first and middle names are both biblical. There is no special implication behind the names other than their biblical roots. Both men were strong characters, and each is remembered in his own way for serving in leadership roles. Stephen was known as the first martyr after being stoned to death, while Andrew was a fisherman with a sterling character who always brought people to Jesus.

My son is now a minister, following his namesakes in Scripture—and his dad!

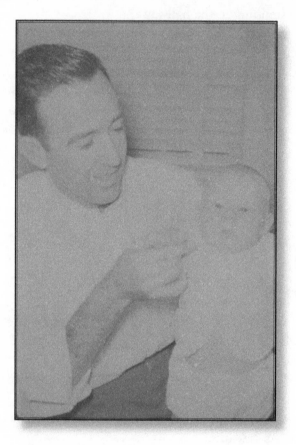

CHAPTER 32

My First Encounter as a Rookie

For the first few months, my responsibilities were very limited. Because of my limited experience, I was shielded from duties for which I had not been trained. I was given light responsibilities in the pulpit on Sunday mornings. I also began compiling a list of prospective members from the visitors pads, Sunday school rolls, and places like city hall where new residents put up their water deposits, along with their church preference.

Most Sunday evenings, I could be found working with youth, a responsibility I had already inherited by doing the same in two previous churches. The pastor knew what he could trust me with, as well as where I needed some tender coaching. Professional skills of the clergy needed tender supervision, but people skills enabled me to come into ministry with a measure of strength.

The church facility where we first worshipped was perhaps seventy to eighty years of age and showed signs of being in a poor state of repair. The sanctuary was a bit antiquated, and the educational area was badly in need of repair and expansion.

The congregation had already purchased some land on the west side of Central Expressway for future relocation. It was exciting to see the church body begin to plan for their future location.

The township of Richardson was at about nine thousand residents when I moved there but on the cusp of an exploding population. Practically all of the new members we received beyond June of 1957 came from the west side of Central Expressway.

Demographers learned that people who lived on the west side also went to church on the west side. Relocation was a must. What the demographers had been predicting absolutely became true.

I have discovered that when one thinks nothing can go wrong, it usually can and does. One morning when I had been in the office for only a short while, my phone rang, and when I answered it, a voice on the other end said, "My child just drowned in the bathtub. Can you come?" Without hesitation, I responded, "Sure!" This was my first emergency response to a tragedy of any kind. As I rushed out to door to go to the residence, I offered a prayer that went something like this: "Lord, I am rushing into a situation that I do not know what to do or how to respond. You must be my very presence in this home."

To this day, I do not remember anything that happened. As I went, the Lord went before me and took complete control of the situation. I know that whatever happened was appropriate, for I became friends with this household. I take no credit for whatever comfort was present and effective in that moment; the only thing I take credit for was the willingness to go in God's name.

I am writing this story to say that it became the capstone to all of my responses in emergency situations—we simply go in God's name and allow God to work through our presence. New experiences, even if they are challenging, can be the ones that make or break the way in which God speaks to us and leads us.

CHAPTER 33

My First Pastorate

I was licensed to preach under the supervision of the late Dr. Wesley V. Hite, superintendent of the Dallas-South district, in the fall of 1956. At the time, I felt a sense of achievement. It was my first step toward earning the role of an elder within the North Texas Conference. (In a way, I was "feeling my oats.")

I look back on it now, and it seems so trivial. But one has to begin somewhere, and this marked my beginning to "wherever." Thank God for the minor victories over the next eight years as I served on the staff of First Methodist Church as their evangelism director—and, loosely speaking, as their assistant minister, liturgist in worship, and funeral (and later wedding) conductor. I organized several adult Sunday school classes and did whatever someone could find for me to do. I also barbered on Saturday. I was a busy fellow but was rewarded enormously.

In 1964, Bob Middlebrooks, the pastor with whom I had worked for several years at Seagoville and Richardson, was appointed superintendent of the Dallas Northeast District during the final stages of a new sanctuary being built. He felt that the bishop could have delayed his new appointment until after the new sanctuary had been opened. He served in his role of superintendent, but his heart ached as pastor.

When Bob left the pastorate to become a superintendent, part of my heart went with him. We had been together in two locations for over ten years, and my mentor and I were separated, outside the womb, and I felt alone in a sea of people.

The new minister who succeeded Bob was a fine man, who treated me with the deepest respect, but a relationship had been disturbed and it was impossible to reconnect in the same way. There was something of the same feeling among the congregation. Many began to turn to me because of my tenure, and I knew it was time for me to move on.

I decided to go see Bob and see if he could find me a new appointment. When I approached him with the idea, he said, "We have only one appointment open, and it is at First Methodist Church in Van Alstyne, Texas. I said, "I'll take it!" He said, "You don't even know where it is located." I replied, "I don't care. I'll take it." He informed me it was in the Sherman district and that I would have to go through Dr. Slack, the superintendent there, in order to be considered.

Bob called Dr. Slack and arranged an appointment, and I went to meet with him at the Grayson Hotel in Sherman to see if there was a possibility of my receiving that appointment. I found Dr. Slack to be rather elusive. After a couple of hours of conversation, he informed me that he would be holding a preacher's meeting in Van Alstyne the following Wednesday. He encouraged me to attend the event, but he failed to mention that I may or may not be the appointee to that charge. I decided to attend the event, just in case I was being considered.

We met in the basement of the Van Alstyne church and went through what I suppose a typical district preacher's meeting was like. I don't remember much about it, so it probably did not amount to much. After the meeting, Dr. Slack took me upstairs into the sanctuary, and to my surprise, most of the members of the official board were there, waiting to meet their new pastor. It was quite a surprise but one that I thoroughly welcomed and enjoyed. I had not ever been given an opportunity like this and considered it a unique honor. I went around and shook hands with each person there, and by the time our meeting was over, I felt as if I had struck a gold mine.

My appointment was effective on February 1, 1965. What a lucky person I was, if *lucky* was the word, to be able to serve a small-town church of approximately two hundred fifty members who were "salt of the earth" type people.

Moving day came quickly, and it was time to get Stephen enrolled into first grade, with Mrs. Ruth Spence as his teacher. Steve fell in love with her immediately and thus started a "love affair" that has lasted some fifty-three years now, if my math is correct. Ruth is now approaching one hundred years of age, is widowed, and lives alone on her farm just north of town.

Lori, my daughter, was not of school age while we were in Van Alstyne, so she spent much of her time entertaining Virginia Ayers and her father, Chili, who lived next door to the parsonage, along with Virginia's friend Joe Baker.

Our youngest child, David, was born at Baylor Hospital in Dallas, as were Steve and Lori. After David's birth, when his mother was ready for discharge, Don Flesher, the funeral director in Van Alstyne, drove the family car used for funeral transportation to Baylor to pick up mother and son. Billie Whitaker made the trip and held David on the return trip.

I have so many memories of Van Alstyne that it would be impossible to rename them. Van Alstyne would have been a great town in which to grow up. It was completely opposite of where I had been living for the previous eight years or so. I had spent my ministry on the fast track, and it seemed extremely relaxing to be able to slow down and smell the proverbial roses.

The congregation treated us with great respect and with small-town cordiality. I loved going to the church early and taking a "time out" during the middle of the morning to walk the two blocks to downtown and have a cup of coffee with the townsfolk and church members alike. City Drug was thegossip center. The main attractions at City Drug were Ruby, Vera Mae, and Sue, the employees who knew not only everyone in town but every*thing* about everyone in town.

The next daily stop was the post office. Between City Drug and the post office, I could encounter the town leaders, town gossipers, and all the community facts I ever wanted to know.

The greatest events of the year came in the fall with the annual football games. Everybody who was anybody showed up at the football games. The town went from full (home games) to empty (away games). The town carnivals were exciting, the American Legion was generally crowded, *The Leader* was well read, the churches were well attended, and the funeral home was busy two or three times a week. The town population was rather static. The announcement of a new family recreation center, or country club, was welcome news.

One of the most grueling jobs I had was writing two sermons a week. The Sunday morning sermon basically took me the better part of five days, and the Sunday evening sermon took me the better part of Sunday afternoon. Sunday was not a day of rest for me; it was a day of labor—delivering on Sunday morning and preparing on Sunday afternoon.

Most of the townspeople were generous to a fault. The Benton's .provided the tennis facilities and the skating rink. City Drug became the gossip center, while the American Legion provided the watering hole. The schools supplied the facilities for just about everything, and the ministerial alliance afforded recreation opportunities for the youth.

Van Alstyne was a great place for my children. The church was the only first pastorate I would ever have. But the only thing I had become accustomed to that it did not have a fast track for me to practice ministry. My soul longed to be back among the suburbanites in an area teeming with people and limitless opportunities. When the opportunity came two short years later, I could not resist, so I accepted an appointment where pastor meets suburbia.

(Disclaimer: I think it inappropriate to discuss any ministerial relationships.)

CHAPTER 34

My Three Children

The mother of my children was sadly killed in an automobile accident in 1979. It was a horrible scene, with three dead, one not expected to live, and two with minor injuries. I was the one not expected to live, but by the grace of God I survived and am in reasonably good health, now eighty-nine years of age.

I cannot say enough to praise my children, not only because of the way they dealt with their mother's death but also by the way they have lived their lives and achieved so much in their careers.

My oldest son is Stephen Andrew Robertson is an ordained United Methodist minister. Steve is married to Connie Bontz. Connie is an able life mate who has energy to burn at a remarkable number of tasks. Connie is an extremely talented person on her own as she works as a secretary to a staff member at St. Andrew United Methodist church in Plano. Connie balances her time between housewife, grandmother and local church activities. Steve and Connie have two children, Jacob and Erin. Jacob is married to Nicki who is a kindergarten teacher in Allen, and they have two children Luke and Benjamin. Erin is employed and is pursuing a degree in nursing. She is planning to wed in May 2020.

My daughter Lori is the middle child, and she married Alan Flores. They have two sons who are loaded with charm and talent. Both boys were diagnosed with Autistic Spectrum Disorder very early on.

Nick is the older of the two, is more social and outgoing than his brother, and graduated from high school in 2018. He has three more years in high school transition classes to develop more daily life skills and to work on vocational training to increase his ability to be employed in the labor force. He is a good-looking young man who shows tremendous promise.

Sam is a more sedate young man of eighteen who graduated in 2019 and has four years of high school transition classes as well. Sam has a wonderful singing voice which he developed from his love of music. He was in the Concert Choir since he was a freshman. Who knows? He may become a recording star down the line.

Alan, my son-in-law, works for Freeman Audio Visual, as did my daughter. Alan has, thirty-five years with Freeman, directly related to the convention and trade show business.

My daughter worked with Freeman for twenty-nine years but was recently laid off due to a reduction in force. I am so proud of what she has done. She has the ability to perform at the highest level and has received many commendations from her company. She has a sweet spirit and is a dedicated worker. She also dedicated 5 years as the President of the Grand Prairie Independent School District Special Education PTA in which she and Alan were very involved.

My third child is a son, David Page Robertson, who is connected with the United Methodist Church of the Resurrection (CORUMC) in Leawood, Kansas, and has worked with Adam Hamilton for something like twenty-four years. Dave is a great pastor and is now linked with a satellite of CORUMC located in Olathe, Kansas. Dave is extremely adept at working with small groups, athletic teams, teaching, counseling, and hosting groups in his home. Dave is a Christ-centered servant who will do anything to encourage individuals and families to become active for Christ and His church. Dave has a most gifted wife Diane Hunter who sings like a canary and organizes activities second to none. They are a beautiful and effective team. They have no children, but they have great fun being together and sharing their servanthood.

I could not be more proud of my children. Perhaps they received their gifts from their mother, but I am around to see them displayed. Thank God for children!

Early 70's.

CHAPTER 35

Texas Veteran's Land Program

My first venture into the market of buying land happened in 1969 when two of my clergy friends and I decided to purchase some acreage through the Texas Veteran's Land Program. Our plan was to search for a tract of land that we could purchase, in a partnership agreement, that was considered affordable and profitable.

One of the partners, Glynn Vickers, Pastor in Celina, Texas began to search which proved both affordable and achievable. Glynn found a track of land fronting Preston Road about two miles North of Gunter, Texas. The farm was one hundred and three acres, with approximately sixty acres across in cultivation and the rest in pasture. Glynn also had a farmer in his church who was willing to lease the farm.

We then made an application to the Texas Veteran's Land Program for a loan of equal amounts to all three applicants. The other applicant was Bob W. Middlebrooks, at that time Superintendent of the Northeast District. One of the comments a member of the Land Board made the remark: "This is peculiar that three preachers have applied to acquire this loan." I ask him, "it isn't illegal is it?' He said: "No, I just had not seen the clergy become involved in the purchase of land."

Once our loan was approved, each of us received a check for then thousand and five hundred dollars. (This was the largest check I had ever received.) The purchase was completed, and we signed a lease to the aforementioned farmer, so he could begin farming the land under cultivation, and he began moving cattle to the pastures.

There was a house on the property which we purchased, so we sold it to a buyer in Gunter and he had the house moved and renovated.

This was a plus that came with the acquisition. So, we continued for a few years simply leasing the property to a farmer and making payments on our loan.

I am not sure of the date, but perhaps in the mid to late 90's we received an offer to purchase the entire track for the price of two thousand five hundred dollars an acre with a signed note of an interest only payment at eleven percent interest.

We had paid three hundred dollars an acre and were turning a profit at twenty-five thousand an acre with an interest only payment for ten years. After the original agreement, at the end of ten years, the purchaser renewed his note at 11% interest with payment (interest) and principle for another ten years.

We went for several years not knowing who purchased our property, but it was disclosed that the purchaser was one of the large automobile dealers – doing a favor for three preachers. What can I say? A blind hog found an acorn.

CHAPTER 36

Southern Methodist University Sports

I enrolled, as a student, in Southern Methodist University for the Spring semester in 1957. I was required to take an entrance exam due to the fact that it had been over eleven years since I had graduated from High School. Having passed the exam, I began my classes on time.

My pastor from Seagoville, First Methodist church, had visited Perkins School of Theology, where I would enroll after completing my under graduate studies, and as far as I understand, shared the knowledge that certain subjects should be studied by me in under graduate school that would be beneficial when I entered the graduate program at Perkins School of Theology. Particular courses for me to include were in philosophy, psychology, sociology, etc.

Also, to make S.M.U. financially possible, I was awarded generous scholarship aid. With S.M.U. being owned by the South-Central Jurisdiction of the Methodist church, I was given adequate recognition of the church-student relationship, but I was required to give back to the university ten hours a week for two years. This was more than a generous offer.

My assignment from the scholarship, placed me in the Vice-President's office at Southern Methodist University, for ten hours a week over four semesters. This assignment placed me with Dr. Sterling Whacker, but under direct supervision from his secretary, first with Nancy Allen and for the second year with Virginia Taylor, whose4 husbands were both Perkins students. Dr. William Tate was the President of SMU and Mrs. Johnnie Marie Grimes was special assistant to President Tate. My duties were varied and extremely rewarding. To be assigned to the university administrative building was an added asset to my classroom studies, and the beginning of building relationships to those in authority.

While I was a student at SMU, I was introduced to what I thought was big time sports. My early time at SMU was when basketball was the sport to watch. Jim Krebs was the height in SMU basketball in more ways than one. Krebs was the closest player to seven feet tall that SMU ever recruited. Through the 1960's basketball flourished with players like Jan Loudermilk, Max Williams, Bob Begert, Gens Elmore, Danny Holman, Bill Ward and Lynn Phillips. These were exciting years.

I remember a few standout football players. The first as Don Meredith, who played high school ball at Mt. Vernon, was inserted into the game against Missouri at half-time trailing I believe 19-0. Bill Meek had developed the "Spread" formation which literally spread the football team practically the width of the football field, leaving the quarterback Meredith and a few linemen in the center of the field with receivers literally from "sideline" to "sideline" giving Meredith the option to run or pass the ball. The "spread" confused the opponents no end. Meredith could option a pass or run. By the end of the game SMU had prevailed by the score of 32-19. Meredith achieved the rank of "All American". Meredith became a prolific passer and was selected by the Dallas Cowboys as the first-round draft pick after his senior year. After years on the gridiron Don excelled in the broadcast booth with Frank Gifford and Howard Cosell. Don stole the show mimicking Willie Nelson with "Turn out the lights…the party's over!" AT the end of his career, when his health was failing, SMU retired his number! He was too ill to come out on the field and accepted the honor while in the broadcast booth.

Other than "Dandy Don" the other high-profile football player was Jerry LeVias, the first African American to play for the Mustangs. LeVias was no doubt the finest receiver ever to play for SMU. Raymond Berry was a receiver years earlier and enjoyed a marvelous career with the Baltimore Colts. Baseball was a sport dropped from competition perhaps in the early 70's!

Golf became one of the varsity sports which saw the rise of Payne Stewart, a "plus-four" phenomenon who was killed in the crash of a Learjet 35 aircraft. The NTSB determined that the crash was due to an incapacitation of the flight crew members due to a loss of cabin pressurization.

CHAPTER 37

The Dalai Lama

The year was 1986, I was the superintende4nt of the Dallas Central district. Dr. Bill Bryan, pastor of Grace United Methodist church in Dallas, called me to announce that he was having a special guest at his church on Monday. He said: "You may want to be here."

I asked: "Who will your guest be?" He said very excitedly: "It is the Dalai Lama!" I responded in a voice as excited as his: "I will definitely be at your church."

The Dalai Lama was beginning a World Tour in order to make his message clear to the people of all nationalities. It was a gigantic effort and we hoped to make him welcome in the city of Dallas and to bless him as he continued his tour.

The Dalai Lama was all that I had imagined him to be, and much more. What does one do in the presence of greatness? I learned quickly that one listens, absorbs and repeats the message at opportunity. The Dalai Lama had a marvelous heart-warming smile that invites him into your world. This event took place over 30 years ago, but I still feel the magnetism of his person.

I actually knew very little about him. He was born in a small rural Chinese village in 1933. Through divine selection he was chosen to be the 14th Dalai Lama. He has spent at least a half-century fulfilling his destiny.

I count this experience to be near the very top of my religious experiences. His life is a prime example of that which he teaches. He has received many awards of significance. In 1989 he was awarded the Nobel Peace prize in recognition of his non-violent behavior.

The Dalai Lama presents an impeccable presence. He is the spiritual leader of the Buddhist movement; he brings a challenge to the whole religious world.

There are at least fourteen major teachings in his presentation. I would like to share with you a brief outline of these teachings.

1. You must understand the law of impermanence. The law states that all sensations are arising and passing away. This includes such things as; happiness, emotions, youth, vigor, suffering, friendship, situations as well as life itself as all arise and pass away.

2. Love and compassion are what we need in the world. Love and compassion are necessities, not luxuries. Without them, humanity cannot survive. We must understand the true nature of each, how they are acquired and how we can properly sustain them.

3. Life is not 'I' and 'mine', it must be 'we' and 'ours'. Scientists agree that people who think in terms of community, have healthier mental lives. All beings want to achieve happiness and await suffering. Perhaps that is why it is better to put yourself in someone else's shoes rather than to play a pat hand. Our prime purpose in life is to help others. If we cannot help them, at least we should not hurt them.

4. Let serving others be your yardstick for happiness. Selfishism is the root for all sin. When we look at others, we recognize the field of our labors. Never be tricked into thinking that self is the way to fulfillment, rather it is the road to ruin. All major religions teach that the way to significance and fulfillment is through others. Invest yourself in those beyond yourself and you will be fabulously wealthy.

5. Construct a view of a shared humanity. To invest in self is to box one in. God did not create us to flourish individually, but He created us to love in a community. Pe3rhaps this is why there are so many fields of education. We are created to be in relation with each other, which finds us sharing the riches od life and the sharing of resources.

6. Recognize the false appearances of things that are unworthy. If any idea can stand alone, or any project has merit of its own we probably have misunderstood it. All things have a dependency

upon other things. The Lone Ranger is a character in a comic book- not a concept for community. If you think you are alone- you are. Let us bond in community so that God's creation can move forward.

7. Break the illusion of self. Our nation is not millions of people wandering alone on this planet. We are made for each other. Life can only be measured if we cross the finish line together.

8. Don't get attached to things. Attributing special values to things makes us desire them, and that leads to greed and dead ends. It is better to remain neutral to things and emotions for that matter. Whether something is valuable or invaluable, negative or positive, always be observant but remain unattached to them. You will save yourself a lot of suffering. We can never alter plans beyond ourselves until we make peace with ourselves.

9. Recognize the interdependence of things. All phenomena are interdependent. There is no good without evil. There is no you without someone else. All problems are more complex than we think. We should never be satisfied with the appearance of things, and more satisfied with the actual. Only the development of compassion and understanding for others can bring us tranquility and happiness we all seek.

10. Concentration brings us closer to the truth. There is a concept known as 'Monkey Mind', which reflects the main operating systems of humanity. We simply come up with a thought and cling to it, then that thought leads to another and another and finally we become lost to the truth. But if you just sit and observe, thoughts arise and pass away. They will lose their power over you.

11. Meditation will lead you into subtler levels of sensations. Each level helps to move you from gross sensation to more subtle levels. If your mind is crowded with thoughts, concentrate on your breath.

12. Self is an illusion. Self is only in your mind. It is a figment of the imagination. We share the planet earth. We must learn to live in harmony and peace with each other and with nature.

13. Mediate on impermanence.

14. Be kind and generous.

CHAPTER 38

It Pays to be Handy

Sometime around the early 1970's, my wife and I decided to purchase some property in the township of Estes Park, Colorado. It had been our custom since the late 1950's and early 60's to spend our vacation in the mountain resort.

Our first visit to Estes Park was a joint venture with the Middlebrook's family, the pastor of the church where I was thus employed. The plan went like this: Bob was to rent a small bumper pulled trailer and take his family to Estes Park, find a camping spot on the Big Thompson River in Devil's Gulch – stay two weeks then we would drive up, stay two weeks and pull the trailer home. The trip was magnificent. Everything went as planned.

The beauty of Estes Park and the aura of the mountains became an obsession. We discovered two different clergy families who owned houses out west of town on the way to the YMCA camp and the entrance into the Rocky Mountain National Park, with highways that went above 12,000 feet altitude until the first snow closed the pass. All two houses, which we alternated on availability, satisfied the needs of our family.

Depending on the age of our children, we used the recreational facilities quite liberally. This was the major vacation spot for us for perhaps 20-25 years. Everything was to our liking.

Then in about 1970 we began to consider purchasing property in that area. Just before we left Estes Park to come home, a particular piece of property, in our price range became available. Our price range was in the low end, and we were particularly attracted to a "seasonal" house and acreage near where we had been staying for several years.

I contacted the Realtor and ask that we may be able to see the house and property. This is what we found. The house was old and very small. This best describes what we saw initially. The living room was approximately 12 x 18' with a large stone fireplace, a small dining room all combined in a family room.

There was a set of stairs that took you to a landing where there is a bath and shower – and down the landing were two small bedrooms, each with bunk beds. Off the living area was a small kitchen with a classic wood cook stove replete with an enclosed hot water heater. Underneath the house was a huge storage area. The property was probably 150-200' deep and perhaps 50-60 feet wide with a small septic tank in the front yard. To say the least, it was an odd home, but with a great location.

There was no financing option in Estes Park, so I decided to pursue that on my return to Texas. Once home, I first went to see my personal banker. He advised me that the bank did not offer any out-of-state loans, but he advised me to approach larger banks in Dallas. On a visit to downtown Dallas I called on an old friend who was Treasurer of the First National Bank of Dallas. I received the same information as from my local banker – no out of state loans!

It seemed that my road had dead ended. The one day I was sharing this story with one of my church members and he said: "I own an Insurance Company in Arizona. I will be glad to see that you receive the appropriate papers to request a loan that could be paid off over the period of a few years". So, we bought the property and went there for a few years as it was, adequate for a few weeks a year in the summer months, and with a little massaging a few days in the winter.

Finally, after three or four years, we decided to modernize and add on. The project was self-realized. I drew up the plans to add a large family room which served as kitchen, dining and lounging area, plus a master bedroom and bath. I took my plans to the city for approval and then begun to work out the construction process. My Dad was a carpenter, while growing up I worked on his job sites several times. With a little knowledge and a gung-ho spirit, with the framing help of an older brother – we went to a large discount lumberyard in Denver and purchased all the materials to get us out of the weather. I must say that by the time we were finished – it looked very much like I envisioned.

One of my brothers was a professional electrician, so I persuaded him to come from New Mexico one weekend and rough in my wiring for the new addition also with the setting of my breaker box, so that I could finish the project before the electrical inspection.

I added several windows along the front of the new construction, plus added outside wood across the front and sides. I did the framing of the roof including reinforcement for the snow fall and anything else the Building Inspector required. Once I was finished with the roofing and the electrical, I called the Inspector and then prepared (when time allowed) to finish the project. It turned out to be much better than I ever dreamed, but the work took much more time.

CHAPTER 39

Big Thompson Flood – 1976

Since we had acquired the Estes Park property, we had found it convenient to make at least a couple of trips each year to our favorite vacation spot.

On this trip, David was working evenings at the Lazy B Ranch which was popular for both a Bar-B-Que dinner and musical entertainment by the Lazy B Wranglers. This as a night we chose not to attend. We dropped David off early in the evening with the intension of picking him up after the show.

At perhaps around 10:00pm we were driving back out to the Lazy B to retrieve our son when we were stopped downtown with water over the roadway. After a telephone call to the Lazy B we were told that everything at their place was fine, and when the water receded, they would bring David home, which they did sometime after midnight.

We had plans the next morning to drive to Denver in order for me to fly to San Francisco to attend a United Methodist church meeting to be held at Glide Memorial United Methodist church in San Francisco. The Reverend Dr. Joseph Washington was to meet me after flying in from Dallas. The meeting was aborted at Glide Memorial because we found the church had been locked because of unusual circumstances.

But the big story was broadcast over my car radio that simply took our breath and imagination away. I would never have believed what I heard over my auto's radio that on the Saturday night of July 31, 1976 a freak storm hit on the Eastern edge of Estes Park and created the historic flood that swept down the Big Thompson canyon in an epic catastrophe that had never been equaled before or since.

I have drawn the information concerning the flood from the meteorologist records substantiated by the local and national weather bureau's which documented the most unusual flood ever to ravage that area.

Strong thunderstorms, fueld by moisture carried by East and Southeasterly winds, developed in the foothills by 6:30pm on July 31, 1976. Over a four- and one-half hour period, heavy rain fell over a 70 square mile area. The most intense rainfall estimated at more than 12 inches occurred over the Western third of the Big Thompson Canyon.

The Big Thompson River and Canyon was susceptible to damaging flash floods. Flooding began just below the town of Estes Park and extended some 25 miles to Loveland, Colorado. The storm developed quickly and fiercely. The peak discharge was 3.8 times the estimated 100-year flood discharge. The flood crested through 7.7 miles in about 30 minutes for an average travel rate of 15 mph.

The river smashed into supports that held up a 227,000-pound water pipe where it crossed the highway. The flood pulled the pipe filled with an estimated 873,000 pounds of water. The damage was unbelievable. The peak stage of the flood was estimated at 19.7 feet.

A reported 3,500 tourists were in the canyon on July 31st preparing to celebrate Colorado's statehood anniversary the following day. Many could not believe the warnings of the State Troopers could possibly be true.

The flood in the Big Thompson Canyon destroyed 316 homes, 45 mobile homes, 52 businesses and 438 automobiles. A total of 143 persons died, five of whom were never found. The property damage was recorded in excess of 35 million.

It has been 43 years since that horrendous flood. I still cannot fully realize the horror of those moments or the vast destruction that took place. From our peaceful little vacation home some 4 miles from the initial rainfall that triggered the consequences – I still cannot fathom the enormity of the events, and even more understand how things on the West side of Estes Park could be so calm, when horrendous catastrophe could befall so many, so quickly.

CHAPTER 40

Citizenship Seminars

I do not remember the precise year, perhaps around 1976 and 1977, that I was the conference clergy selected to lead a group of seventy high school seniors along with perhaps fifteen adult counselors on a few days trip to Washington DC followed by a four day trip to the United Nations in New York City. This was a time to become acquainted with the structure and function of government in Washington DC and to spend time with the international community of nations in New York City.

The time of the year must have been during the mid-term break, for it was in the period of winter that enhanced our trip so much. Cold enough to have snow, but not too cold to be able to frolic in it somewhat.

We flew from DFW airport directly to Friendship Airport in Baltimore, Maryland. When we landed, we were greeted with perhaps 6-8" of snow on the ground, but none falling as we landed. We boarded busses and proceeded immediately to Mount Vernon, one-time estate of our first President, George Washington. I was as thrilled as were the high school students, for I had never been to either of our destinations.

While on Washington we were given a tour of the White House and during our time there we sat in on a convened meeting of the senate and the House of Representatives at the capitol building. We were not privileged to witness the passage of any bills into law but we were able to see our congress persons at work, listening and debating the pros and cons. Mostly our one-on-one experiences was simply to see our elected officials at work and to learn what the current events were in Washington that might interest the voting public.

We were fortunate, in most instances, to meet with our elected officials representing our local precincts back home. Putting names and faces together was a huge thrill. Washington is a busy place, and we quickly learned that we may be in personal conversation, when our representative or senator excused themselves to go vote for/against a bill being considered. I think our tour group really appreciated the 'exchange' of meeting with a real live congressman or senator.

We were able to sit in on a case under review with the Supreme Court. To know and be reassured that we are a people protected by law is reassuring and that all things are reviewed in the light of its constitutional status.

From Washington we flew into New York City and were housed in a hotel very near the United Nations complex. Our schedule had been worked out in advance of our visit. The next morning was very special, in that we were able to meet with George Herbert Walker Bush, then the United States Ambassador to the United Nations and later to become President of the United States.

On that given morning when Ambassador Bush was to address our group, he brought two foreign ambassadors with him. The total group was excited. When Ambassador Bush stepped up to the microphone to spe4ak, one of our students raised her camera to get her intended pictures. When she pushed the button her flash bulb exploded with a deafening sound, at which time the Ambassador fell to the floor, as if this had been rehearsed. The whole audience was relieved to know it was a flash bulb not an assassin's bullet! What a relief! Drama without negative results.

It was a total surprise for us, as we were scheduled to attend Radio City Music Hall that we were treated to the premier of Jesus Christ Superstar. What an extravaganza! The production was beautifully done even though it was a controversial production, it was well choreographed, and the costumes were extravagantly made. All the members of our party were thrilled with the show.

To our surprise, while we were in the theater, we must have had two to three inches of fresh snow fall. The group walked from Radio City Music Hall to the hotel. The temperature was conducive to our walking – and it was enjoyed by all.

CHAPTER 41

Superintendent to Pastorate

In 1977, I had been serving as the superintendent of the Dallas South District for almost four years. I had fifty-eight churches assigned to my district: metropolitan, suburban, and rural churches. The travel throughout my district was tiresome, and in most evenings I was required to be away from my family. The schedule became exhausting. I had three children still at home, and I longed to be a greater part of their lives, their school functions, and our family life.

My presiding bishop was forced to be out of town for several days to attend meetings with some of our general agencies. He asked me to meet him at the airport when he returned. When we were leaving the airport, he asked how the most recent appointments had gone. I referred to three churches in particular from which pastors had been reassigned and other pastors were taking their place. One of our megachurches needed to have its pastor position filled because the pastor had been reassigned to the faculty of our seminary at SMU. The other church was in a critical suburban area. The moves had left a church open in the northern part of our conference, near Lake Texoma. The church was Waples Memorial United Methodist in Denison, Texas, a congregation of about twelve hundred parishioners.

It was an enticing opportunity for me that would provide some relief from grueling work on the district, as well as fill a pastoral void for which I was originally called and missed so dearly. I made my pitch for the appointment, and the bishop said that he would consider it and let me know within a brief span of time.

The bishop called me in a couple of days and said that he had approved the appointment, effective December 1, 1977, with the stipulation that I complete my charge conferences. These required my presence as the district superintendent, who was the presiding officer in every local church, as they conducted their year-end reporting along with a celebration of their accomplishments. The conference provided a way for the superintendent to congratulate them on their past year's work and present them with a challenge for the future. I cannot tell you how much it means for a congregation to celebrate its true achievements over the past twelve months and to begin a new year on a positive note. I love to play the role as a "conference cheerleader" as a local church catches a glimpse of their tremendous opportunities for the upcoming year.

Given my responsibilities for December 1977, I still had at least fifteen churches to visit in order to preside over their charge conferences, on top of preaching each Sunday morning at Waples and fulfilling some duty each day before I began my drive to the next conference.

I do not want you to feel that I was working under an unfair demand or situation. It was a God-given challenge, and I reveled in it. To be with people and to celebrate their successes is a celebration for all. Wherever people are, I feel that is where God is, and that is a place I enjoy.

I looked upon 1978 with great excitement. I had inherited a good and dedicated staff who welcomed me with open arms, and we worked together under a single purpose—to serve the needs of our congregation. Rolly Walker was serving as an assistant pastor while attending Perkins School of Theology, giving perhaps twenty hours a week of his time to various responsibilities, both assigned and volunteering.

My other clergy staff member, with remarkable gifts in every area of ministry, was Paul Cardwell. He served with distinction for years in the office as the director of Christian education for the annual conference. Paul was an invaluable resource in that field. What a pleasure it was to have someone with that knowledge and status on staff.

It was a great surprise to me that on my first Monday of work, Paul came in and handed me his letter of resignation. I was beyond words. How could this happen to me? To lose a man of such character and distinction was more than I could bear. I asked him why, and he replied that he thought every pastor should have the right to name his own staff.

After he walked out of my office, I immediately drafted a letter to him indicating that I desired his presence on our staff and that there was no one I would rather have than him. I felt that he was the best authority in Christian education within and without the boundaries of the annual conference. I pleaded with him to reconsider his resignation and join me in the work at Waples. To my great pleasure, he responded positively. He simply said that he felt he should be invited, rather than assume he still had the responsibility. I have never forgotten that experience, and it was a learning time for me.

I also inherited an experienced secretary who knew everyone connected to our congregation, and what a blessing it was to have her introduce all of her acquaintances to me. A pastor who does not know his parishioners is pastor to none.

With time came inevitable changes. One of the first staff changes came when the business manager indicated that he must resign because he was moving out of the state. This was a blow to me because I had never even seen the books. I assume he could have nurtured me along from the time I came, but my interests were on general management and my own need to be a pastor to the people and a shepherd to the flock.

Therefore, one of my first duties was to find a replacement for my business manager. After much prayer and deliberation, I decided to go after Reverend Ken Summy, who was a retired navy chaplain living in Whitesboro, Texas, not a far commute from our church. I had met Ken at a district meeting and was very impressed with his manner of dress and demeanor.

So, about midmorning one day, I drove over to Whitesboro, met Ken and his wife, and had a very nice discussion in their home. I introduced the reason I had come to see him, and frankly I was surprised at his response. He said that he was not interested in the position but appreciated the offer. I was disappointed in his response and a bit taken aback that I had been refused. (I don't take refusals lightly.) I excused myself and drove back to Denison very dissatisfied.

I took a couple of days to think about his refusal and decided that I wasn't convinced that he was that definite. There was something unexplainable about our conversation, which I replayed over and over in my head. Since I could not clear it out of my mind, I made a decision to drive back over to Whitesboro and give him one more effort. I found him outside feeding his livestock. I parked my car and walked over to where he was. We exchanged cordial greetings, and I simply said, "Ken, I need you!" And to my pleasant surprise, he said, "When do you want me to start?" Short, simple, effective!

I also had lost my student associate, who, upon graduation, wanted to go back to Louisiana from which he had come. I worked with the bishop to find a replacement. I interviewed two different candidates, after which I asked Bishop Stowe if he would appoint Carroll Caddell as associate minister to Waples. He did, and my staff was once more complete.

After about two years, Ken Summy was forced to retire, so the search was on again. My intuition led me to explore someone I had known years before at First UMC in Richardson. He had been the business administrator for the Richardson Independent School District for several years before he entered the pastoral ministry. He was currently serving as the superintendent of the Wilmer-Hutchins Independent School District, a district that had encountered much turmoil over the preceding years. I drove down to Wilmer and approached Alden "Chubby" Armstrong about moving to Denison. He practically leaped into my arms with great joy, and without hesitation he accepted the position.

So, once again, I had a complete staff and all looked well.

Wrong! Soon after, I suffered the greatest tragedy of my lifetime. My wife and I and my two associates and their wives were involved in an automobile accident as we turned off the highway and onto a street that led us to the Armstrongs' home. We were blindsided by a drunk driver who was traveling at an estimated speed of ninety-five miles per hour, killing three people instantly. Those killed were my wife and both of the Armstrongs. I was seated in the left back of the automobile, but with the car so damaged, the first responders had to remove my body through the back glass.

Of course, I was unconscious for most of three days. The physicians told my family on the first day that I would more than likely not live through the night. On the third day I was in intensive care my son Steve and daughter Lori came in to see me. I asked them where was

Mom and when they couldn't answer me and I looked into their eyes I realized that she had died. Bishop Stowe and his wife Twila were on vacation in Nova Scotia, and upon learning of the accident, they came home to minister to the needs of my family and staff. What a dear couple they were!

By this time, my oldest son, Stephen, was in college in Georgetown, Texas; Lori was studying criminal justice at Grayson County College; and David was in the ninth grade. These were traumatic times within our family, but the church family and many friends provided comforting support. The larger family can enable us to survive and grow through most tragedies.

CHAPTER 42

Automobile Accident

It was September 10, 1979 when I awakened for a moment, in the Intensive Care Unit of the Texoma Medical Center in Denison, Texas. A medical doctor stood over my bed and was telling me that he was going to do something in my stomach, after which I lost consciousness again.

I later found out that I had been in an automobile accident a few hours before along with my wife, two of my Associate Pastors and their wives. The six of us were in an automobile driven by Associate Pastor Carroll Caddell. The passengers in the automobile included: Carroll's wife Carolyn, Associate Pastor Alden Armstrong and his wife Georgia Raye, myself and my wife Eppie. Pastor Armstrong, his wife and my wife were killed instantly. Pastor Caddell and his wife were not injured seriously, and that I was not expected to love through the first night.

The Doctors took approximately one hundred stitches to bind the head wounds. I had a broken pelvis and multiple other wounds. What bothered me was the undetermined.

I was still in ICU when I learned that my wife had been killed. My older son Steve was in Southwestern University in Georgetown, Texas. My daughter Lori had just finished High School and was planning to go to Grayson County Community College to study Criminal Justice. David, my youngest, just finished the ninth grade. My home was empty. No father to administer the household. No mother at all. Thank God, I had family who were able and willing to come and stay for a few days and help with my children.

To compound the issue, the Pastor of the church (me) was incapacitated for a lengthy period, one of the Pastors (Business Manager, dead), the other associate is wanting to move. The staff is decimated, who is in charge? Who is going to preach? My plate was running over and no one in sight to make and monitor decisions.

I remained in ICU for 3 more days, after that I was placed in a patient room with someone from my church with me as many days as I needed them. But I was incapable of making decisions about my family or the church for essentially three weeks, at which time I was able to go home, if, I had a hospital bed delivered to my home.

While I was still in the hospital, I had been on my back for days. One night late, a church member Brett Swain was with me for four hours. I remember saying to Brett; "I need to get on my stomach." He said; "How are we going to manage that?" I said; "I will take the handrail on the side of my bed and will pull myself up as far as I am able and then you reach under me and slip me on my stomach." So, I did as I told him and when I was up as far as I could pull myself, I said; "okay Brett, now!" Being a stout man, he flipped me like a sack of flour. As soon as I was on my stomach, the pain increased, and I said; "Okay Brett, turn me back over." A worthy experiment turned sour!

My Associate who was driving the car came to me and said thay he felt he needed to move to another appointment. He felt guilty for being the driver of the car in which three persons were killed, although I assured him that the blame was not on his shoulders. But nothing seemed to make him feel better, so I wished him well and seldom saw him after that.

I had a retired clergyman who had been on staff but long retired, helped us enormously. But age and health prevented him from diving in and helping out for any period of time. But the name of Paul Cardwell will live long in the history of this account.

The accident happened in late September 1979, but it was months before I could get adequate replacements. The next Spring, I received a telephone call from my Bishop. He said that there was a man graduating from Iliff Seminary in Denver at the end of the Spring semester and could be available to come to Waples in May of 1980 if I wanted to call him. I did call him, and he sounded positive about my invitation. So, I met him in Dallas and brought him up to Waples. It was a positive experience, so I ask the Bishop to appoint him to Waples at the end of the semester. His name was Dennis Wilkinson.

Then I picked up the name of another clergy, a retired Lt. Colonel retired from the Air Force by the name of Ken Summy. Ken lived in Whitesboro, some 25-30 miles away. I drove over to Whitesboro within the next few days and invited Ken to join our staff. Ken was not positive about the move, therefore I returned to Denison extremely disappointed. Within a very short time I decided to go back and see Ken. When I saw him, I said" Ken I need you to accept this job!" Without hesitation he said; "When do I start?"

I had struck pay dirt! Two wonderful men – two new staff members. The Lord looks out for his own. The two men came joyfully and brought with them credentials beyond question. What a great staff we had and with church Secretary Jean Caldwell things could not have been better.

To ice the cake, Jane and I set our wedding day for May 30, 1980. I contacted Bishop Stowe to perform our wedding to which he agreed, and things were looking good again.

Shortly after this, a lady from our congregation came to me, the wife of a prominent physician, and informed me that she would like to design and make a complete set of liturgical hangings for our sanctuary as a gift of love. She shared the design and colors for the Advent Season of that Fall. They were beautiful in every aspect and true to the Season of Advent. I brought the idea forward to our congregation. There was one objection, from a very staunch and long-time member. I said to him; "I will make you a deal. Let's install the first set of Banners for Advent. If we have significant objection, I will halt the process. If we do not, we will accept her offer". He agreed, and the congregation was elated.

Before the next conference year, my resident Bishop called and asks if I would be willing to be appointed Superintendent of the Dallas Central District in the conference year of 1982. After thinking about it I called him and said; "If it were possible could he delay the appointment until 1983?" The reason being that my youngest son needed until that time before he graduated from High School. The Bishop agreed, so in 1983 Jane and I moved to Dallas.

CHAPTER 43

A Marriage Made in Heaven

Some time later, I married Jane Hynds Benton on May 31, 1980, in a lovely ceremony performed by Bishop W. McFerrin Stowe in the beautiful sanctuary of Waples Memorial United Methodist Church in Denison, Texas. It was the celebration of all celebrations since I had been their pastor. I was bringing to the parsonage a new wife since my first wife had been killed the year before. The hymn that Jane and I chose for our wedding is following.

> Praise to the Lord, the Almighty, the King of Creation!
> O my soul, praise him, for he is thy health and salvation!
> All ye who hear, now to his temple draw near;
> Join me in glad adoration!
>
> Praise to the Lord, who o'er all things so wondrously reigning
> Bears thee on eagles' wings, e'er in his keeping maintaining.
> God's care enfolds all, whose true good he upholds.
> How hast thee not known his sustaining?
>
> Praise to the Lord, who doth prosper they work and defend thee;
> Surely his goodness and mercy here daily attend thee.
> Ponder anew what the Almighty can do,
> Who with his love doth befriend thee.

Praise to the Lord, who doth nourish thy life and restore
thee,
Fitting thee well for the tasks that are ever before thee.
Then to thy need God as a mother doth speed,
Spreading the wings of grace o'er thee.

Praise to the Lord! O let all that is within me adore him!
All that hath life and breath, come now with praises
before him!
Let the amen sound from the people again:
Gladly forever adore him.

The hymn filled the sanctuary as our hearts soared in the love we had committed one to the other. There was no doubt in either mind that God had brought us together and would be our constant companion.

The reception that followed was an endorsement of our union and the affirmation of the congregation that they were united as one behind our divine marriage. What a true witness it was to what God can do to those who love Him and each other.

Everything went perfectly from beginning to end. We will always be grateful to Bishop and Twila Stowe, the choir, the organist, the ushers, and others who participated.

Jane and I went out to Tanglewood Resort to spend our wedding night in one of their large tower suites. We went back to Waples on Sunday morning so that I could preach and then began our drive to Estes Park, Colorado, for our honeymoon. What an exciting moment that was for both of us. I was eager to show Jane all of the sites around the Rocky Mountain National Park, my cabin, and the friends we had come to love—but not nearly as eager as I was to be away with Jane for a couple of weeks. New, intimate relationships require a great deal of tenderness and special care, and I especially wanted to be aware of her feelings and needs. We felt we were created for each other; therefore, whatever we did seemed natural and pure.

Of course, our marriage took on special responsibilities because of our children. To develop a relationship with a wife is one thing; to learn how to relate to adult children is something else. One does not automatically assume a parental role because one has to first learn to relate as adult to adult within a family setting while also learning how to relate as more mature adults, offering whatever resources are at our command, without being superior or demanding. I think the spouse's children can be resistant to what is intended as advice. If there is an unresolved issue, perhaps it should first be discussed with the spouse, and then he or she should visit with his or her children as an intercessory action before proceeding with a designed plan. This is tedious work and requires the best of us to execute it.

Jane has two children, Kay and Bill, from her first marriage to Henry Benton, who died an untimely death in 1966. His father had started an insurance business, and after World War II he took it over. After his death, Jane assumed the management of the agency for fourteen years until our marriage, when her son, Bill, took ownership of the agency and has managed it with meticulous precision. Bill and his wife, Paula, are both in the real estate business as well. They have three children, Kathryn who was diagnosed with Angelman's Disease at an early age, Henry who is an attorney and James is working with a private telephone company. Henry and his wife Hayden have a son George and James and his wife Jessica have a son named Mason,

Kay and her husband, Bill Stuart, live in Steamboat Springs, Colorado, where they owned a grocery and wine store for over twenty years. They are both retired from full-time employment and now work part-time with SKI Corp. They enjoy their winter home but also own a condominium in Dallas, where they spend several months each year. They are a delightful couple with whom we enjoy whatever time we have together. Blending families is never an easy thing to do, but it was not too difficult for Jane and me because our children were mature and perhaps understand what it would mean to lose one's mate. There have been cordial relationships on both sides for thirty-seven years now. Living alone is not easy, while marriage provides satisfying relationships in all quarters. To get married after the loss of a spouse depends upon the love of two people and their willingness to make whatever adjustments are necessary.

After our wedding, Jane and I remained in Denison from 1980 until 1983, at which time Bishop John Russell asked me to become superintendent of the Dallas Central District, which had offices downtown in the First United Methodist Church building at Ross and Harwood. There was no district parsonage, so we bought a condominium in North Dallas, and I drove downtown every day. The Dallas North Tollway was new, and the traffic was accommodating. I could get to my office within about twenty minutes at the most. This was the first time we had lived alone since our marriage, and we loved where we lived. Life was good.

However, I missed the local church. The people at Denison had been so good to us, and being a local church pastor was the height of my calling. But it felt good being back on a district. The responsibilities between being a pastor and a superintendent are so diverse that it is exhilarating and often more challenging. I had about thirty churches assigned to my district. There was a great deal of travel involved, but most of the churches were within twenty or so miles.

CHAPTER 44

The Making of a Movie

In 1984 Jane and I accompanied the Reverend Dr. Don Benton and his wife Rosie on a trip to Baltimore, Maryland to attend the General Conference of the United Methodist Church in celebration of it's 200th anniversary. A fabulously historic moment in the life of our church.

As a side trip we decided to go to Williamsburg, Pennsylvania to enjoy the wonders of this historic village. It was a marvelous trip which we have recalled many times, and while there we were introduced to an opportunity of a lifetime. Don and Rosie were in the process of developing a motion picture based on a book that had been written by a sister of an employee of Don's church, Lovers Lane United Methodist Church of Dallas, Texas. The book title, and subsequently the title of the movie was, "Papa was a Preacher." The lead character was "Pop" Porter, a retired pastor from North Texas well into his 90's.

Jane and I were enthralled with the idea and subsequently pledged to invest as much as $25,000 in the project. We were brought into the conversation about all the plans that had been made, of which we were thrilled. This was the beginning of a new adventure for Jane and me. To be in production of a movie was a thrilling adventure. Don and Rosie were excited about us being involved, and we were riding the clouds of a fresh new enterprise.

Jane and I were informed that Don and Rosie had contacted a well-known movie producer in Hollywood by the name of Martin Jurow to produce this film. Mr. Jurow had recently produced two highly successful films, "Breakfast at Tiffany's" and "Terms of Endearment." He sounded like a natural for "Papa was a Preacher." Mr. Jurow was very complimentary concerning the script of the subject matter. He said, "It was written for success." He thought the film would go well.

All the cast was selected, everyone appeared to be pleased, so very soon the movie went into production. One of the early buildings to be used was First Methodist Church in Hutchins, Texas just southeast of the metroplex off Interstate 45.

Some of the investors attended portions of the filming. Jane and I stayed far away. The pastor of the church in Hutchins complained to Mr. Jurow that some of the film crew were smoking on church property. The filming was not interrupted, however.

There was a beautiful and tasteful dinner served at a ranch North of Dallas on the culmination of the filming and the Reverend Dr. Benton staged a delightful "cutting horse" contest in the enclosed arena at the ranch. The premier showing of "Papa was a Preacher" took place at the Inwood Theater in Dallas and the spotlights filled the air as the investors and movie goers celebrated this initial event. What a thrill it was for Jane and me to become involved in other enterprises!

CHAPTER 45

Unorthodox Way to Build a Vacation Home

What could have been the beginning of a few days of a relaxing vacation in Pagosa Springs, Colorado actually turned into the most unorthodox way to actually build a vacation home. Plan on the ordinary but turn your imagination loose and see what can happen in two days.

Jane's brother Robert, along with other parties owned a home five miles East of Pagosa Springs in an area known as San Juan River Resorts. His home was one of several which had been built several years ago, and now the house was aging and in need of repair, although we thoroughly enjoyed our accommodations.

We toured the area freely and enjoyed greatly a trip to Durango with a visit to the Mesa Verde National Park and specifically to the Cliff Dwellings. Jane and I both enjoy historic sites and, in our life, together have visited numerous. Also North of Mesa Verde was a narrow-gauge Railway that would take you to several mountain villages. Although we chose to skip the "Narrow Gauge" we had a grand outing. Every day was filled with new sites of interest and views of the magnificence of Southwest Colorado.

As our vacation time was winding down, a marvelous idea came to mind. This was such a beautiful part of the United States, we would certainly come back here again and again. Then the idea took root and we entertained the thought "why not build a vacation home in Pagosa Springs?" So much to do, so little time! But once the idea has been turned loose, we decided to go with it.

Our minds were working together perfectly. We know what we wanted, why not achieve the impossible? We had two days left of our vacation. Why not use them creatively and fully. All we needed to do was to find and purchase the perfect lot on which we would build our vacation home. The next morning, we went to one of the local Realtors and asked about the availability of a lot on which we might have a house built.

The Realtor showed us a few lots on a "drive-by" until she showed us a lot in a cul-de-sac where there were perhaps eight or ten houses. We found the view of a mountain range from the lot very attractive, so we entered into a contractual agreement and purchased the lot. The area surrounding the lot was filled with trees and shrubs.

The next thing we needed to do was to find a builder who would accommodate our needs. While traveling the highway on the West side of Pagosa Springs we had seen a sign of a company who built log homes. The idea of a log home was intriguing. So, we stopped by their sales office and met the owner of the company, Terry Smith whose father Alton, worked with him. After a couple of hours discussing what we would like to have built, he loaded us up with several magazines of floor plans.

Terry said to us that he and his father were lessors of a small motion picture theater in the township of Pagosa Springs. He asked us to browse the magazines and see if we could find something of interest. If we did why don't we come to the theater in the evening and let him see what we were thinking. Terry was in the projection booth with equipment that ran with little attention, so he could devote adequate time to understand what we wanted. We discussed the project for a couple of hours and Terry said: "If you can meet me for breakfast in the morning, I will have your plans completed".

We met him for an early breakfast before we started back to Dallas. When we saw his plans, we were elated. We signed a contract and drove home. Project completed! We did not go back to Pagosa Springs until our house was finished. We had an account from which Terry could draw funds to satisfy his financial needs. He sent us photo's every few days to let us see the house as it matured.

Your cup of tea? Perhaps not but for us it worked beautifully. We not only had a new home, but we also made a friend for life. We kept the place for several years before selling it and building a new home in McKinney.

P.S. Want to know a little about the house? It was built on a lot in the cul-de-sac facing the mountain range. The home was two story made of brown logs, with the upper story containing the master bedroom upstairs with a nice bath. A hallway led into a large multipurpose room of kitchen, dining and living room with a beautiful wood stove for heat. At the very front of the upstairs was an outside porch, complete with a wooden swing which seated two persons. An area as wide as the house and some 10' of space for the pleasure of sitting outside.

The ground floor consisted of three bedrooms, with bath, and a one car garage included. There was an outside stairwell leading into the living area, and a stairwell downstairs linking the bedrooms to the living room.

CHAPTER 46

An Experiment with the Mormon Tradition

In 1963 the General Board of Evangelism within the Methodist denomination invited 40 clergymen from across the United States, to conduct an experiment in the hope of generating an interest in Methodism in a city largely dominated by the church of Latter-Day Saints, better known as Mormons.

Of the 40 clergymen attending, four of us were senior class members from Perkins School of Theology at Southern Methodist University in Dallas, Texas. Each of us was issued material in advance of our visit that related to the history of the early development of the Mormon tradition which began in New York State and moved Westward across the Northern states to finally settle in the state of Utah, where they made their permanent home. Joseph Smith was the original founder of the religious movement, claiming he had found some 'Gold Tablets' which contained the revelation concerning the theology and philosophy of their new religion.

As the founders moved Westward by wagon train, Joseph Smith was murdered in Illinois, therefore they chose a new leader, Brigham Young who continued westward until they reached a mountain overlook of the Salt Lake valley, in which Brigham Young made the declaration: "This is the place!" A huge plaque rests there today and this is where they settled down.

We four Perkins scholars drove by car to Salt Lake City excited to be part of this noble mission. We were there for two weeks attempting to satisfy the goals for which we went. Our leader was the Reverend Doctor

Lawrence Lacour, Executive Director of the Board of Evangelism in Nashville, Tennessee.

Our routine went something like this; In the mornings we attended classes led by Dr. Lacour concerning the history and doctrine of the Mormon tradition; in the afternoons the students visited door to door; in the evenings there was a revival at the First Methodist Church the first week, and a revival at the only other Methodist church in the city the second week. In the evenings the students would go into the homes of the members, two by two, and hold cottage meetings in the nature of why we were there in the first place.

In addition to these activities we were given tours of the city and attended more seminars on the breadth of the Mormon traditions. The Methodists and other non-Mormon groups were largely under siege from the Mormons. It was difficult to maintain a positive presence, for the Mormons were not friendly with our mission, although the people were friendly, they have a distain for opposing views. Personally, I do not consider the Mormons to be very orthodox in their beliefs.

All of the students spent their afternoons visiting door to door in the residential neighborhoods. I never failed to get a reply from a knock on the door. Each visit with a Mormon family was cordial and rather pleasant, however never once did I get an invitation to enter the home. We were asked, before we left the residence to read a brief passage of scripture and offer a brief prayer. The Mormons were generally receptive to our visit but not exuberant.

On some of the afternoons we were given tours of different buildings near the Temple. The Temple is off limits to some of the Mormons, especially to non-Mormons.

One of the interesting features of the City of Salt Lake is that it is a perfect grid with streets running one direction and avenues running parallel in the other direction. Easy directions. One can literally be at 3rd street and 3rd avenue. Many of the streets are exceedingly wide. One man described it this way: The streets were built so that a person could turn a team of horses around in the middle of the street or take your pick, so that Brigham Young children could not throw rocks at each other.

The way I see the Salt Lake City experiment was just that – an experiment with little to gain. The Mormons are in control of the city and have never budged one bit in truly allowing religious freedom to dwell within their gates. But it was a marvelous experience for me.

CHAPTER 47

Origin and Development of CareFlite

When a seed is planted, who can envision the end result? One of the most dynamic developments to come out of my era is the innovation and creation of CareFlite. CareFlite was officially established in 1979. It is the oldest joint use of air medical transportation service in the United States.

But what was the actual genesis of CareFlite? Whose brainchild was it? I have read the latest information on CareFlite as of September 18, 2019. It is an amazing program, developed far beyond the earliest visions of the possibilities I remember. I am approaching 90 years of age. I was perhaps in my 50's when I first heard about this fabulous program. My memory has played tricks on me from time to time, but this is what I remember.

Because I was an ex-official member on the Board of Methodist Hospital in Dallas, by virtue of my office as Superintendent of the Dallas South District of the United Methodist Church. Living in boundaries of the North Texas Conference, my office entitled me to 'voice and vote'. When I first heard about the possibilities of CareFlite, I believed we dismissed a joint venture with the John Peter Smith Hospital in Fort Worth. There may have been the talk of including the Dallas area hospitals, city and church related as well. But when the dust settled, the program was much larger than earlier dreamed. But isn't that the way many programs begin? I find that I was extremely fortunate to have been in that place at that time. I only had voice and 1 vote yet look at the result of our corporate thinking.

Let me fast-forward some 45 years to 2019 and share with you. Something of the current state of this remarkable innovation. CareFlite is a Texas, 501(C)3 nonprofit corporation sponsored by Baylor Scott and White, John Peter Smith Health Network, Methodist Health Systems, Parkland Health and Hospital and Texas Health Resources. CareFlite and its aggregate body is the only fully integrated medical transport company serving North Texas. It offers medical transport in helicopter, an airplane and ground ambulances. It also provides wheelchair transport. Services are provided by over 700 EMS professionals.

From one helicopter in 1979 transporting about 20 patients each month, CareFlite now operates 6 helicopter bases in and around the Dallas/Fort Worth metroplex including McKinney, Gainesville, Granbury and Whitney. In addition to the helicopters CareFlite has fixed wing, twin engine, pressurized, high performance turbo prop air ambulances for emergency transports in Texas and Oklahoma, as well as, long haul transfers throughout the continental U.S. CareFlite has transported over 1,150,000 patients by air and by ground.

CareFlite responds to requests from hospitals, fire departments, EMS agencie4s and law enforcement within an area of more than 100 counties in a 150-mile radius of the Dallas/Fort Worth metroplex containing more than 7 million people.

CareFlite offers annual emergency care operations each May to first responders and health care professionals. It even has a bicycle team for community events and a mounted team. CareFlite's continuing education programs include year-round certification courses at its Mabee EMS Training Center in Grand Prairie as well as the University of Maryland Critical Care Paramedic Course and the Emergency Medical Dispatch course from the International Academy of Emergency Dispatch (IAED)

If you are interested in more information, go to this link: https://www. careflite.org/cfdocs/CareFlite-History-2019.pdf

Additional Information:

1979 – CareFlite begins with 1 helicopter and transported about 100 patients with a staff of 15 employees.

1980 – 327 patients flown, a 2nd helicopter was purchased, and ground ambulance service was established.

1982 – First emergency care update conference held.

1986 – CareFlight was established in Sydney, Australia after visiting CareFlite in Dallas-Fort Worth.

1989 – 10th anniversary, CareFlite flew 6,563 patients in the first 10 years.

1990 – Purchased 4 more helicopters and completes 14,000th medical flight.

1992 – Builds hanger and dispatch at the Grand Prairie Airport and obtains FAA air carrier certificate.

2004 – Completes 70,000th air medical missions.

2009 – Over 475,000 patients are transported in total including over 80,000 by air.

2014 – Over 750,000 total patients have been transported since 1979.

2019 - 40th Anniversary 1,178,357 total patients since 1979. 375,287 CareFlite Members. 661 Employees.

CHAPTER 48

The Shadow Sides of the Church

Case 1

I served three different special appointments during my ministerial career. I consider myself fortunate to have been selected to serve these4 special appointments, although I found that I was not always equipped to handle each and every situation but discovered there were resources available that enabled me to be just in every situation.

One case came to my office by a young woman who claimed she had been sexually molested by her pastor. I asked her if she could in any way be mistaken about the circumstances involving her person? She stated precisely what the violation involved and according to human judgement, her pastor had crossed the line of propriety.

After her visit to my office, I called my Bishop and shared the precise circumstances with him. The Bishop advised me to select one of the other Superintendents and for the two of us to confront the pastor in question considering his violation of human conduct.

The pastor in question denied any immoral behavior and told me that he would like to meet with her in an attempt to clear his name. I told him that he was forbidden to make any contact with her whatsoever!

After sleeping on the matter, I decided to call the abused woman and ask her to meet with me again the next day, this time I would get her to provide me with a written account of what she had shared with me verbally. I was never able to talk with her again. She had suddenly disappeared and no one in the congregation could verify whatever happened to her.

No doubt in my mind but that the pastor accused had contacted her and had pleaded with her to discontinue her quest for justice. Money could have changed hands, but I will never know. But I did have another visit with the pastor in question and assured him that he would constantly be monitored with regard to any case where there could have been an impropriety.

Case 2

I received a phone call from my Bishop informing me of the facts about a so-called incident. The perpetrator was not young and perhaps uniformed, rather he was older if not wiser. The clergy involved was single and was at a private tennis facility near Austin. The complainant was a lady who was a member within the Episcopal area of our resident Bishop. The Bishop was referring the matter to me to me handled judiciously.

I called the clergy and informed him of the nature of the complaint. Basically, the accuser was a guest of the tennis facility. She had accused the clergy of drinking, using unsavory words, telling risqué stories, and basically brash in his behavior. A true veteran in his social behavior.

I know the person well and I accepted his statement with skepticism. I was neither the judge nor the accuser, I was simply the one who was given the authority to explore the situation, and if necessary, share my findings with the Bishop who initiated my involvement.

When I called the Bishop, he said immediately: "Forget the whole thing!" The woman's husband called and said "my wife saw nothing, heard nothing and tells nothing. Case closed!"

So, in a situation where little could happen, nothing did! An exercise in futility.

Case 3

The cabinet for the North Texas Conference was comprised of: Bishop for the Episcopal area, seven District Superintendents, Council on Ministries Director and the Director of Church Development. At the time of this incident we were in session at Highland Park United Methodist church in Dallas.

Word came early that morning that the wife of one of our clergy had been deliberately attacked in the garage of their home in the early hours of the day at hand. The information concerning the attack was incomplete and the condition of the wife was unknown, but the whole report was bizarre and incomplete. I said to the Bishop: "If you will excuse me, I feel that I need to be at the hospital to offer prayers for her and to be the front-line support for her husband." The Bishop excused me and urged me to stay in touch with him and keep him informed of the situation.

It was roughly 10:00am when I arrived at the hospital, I went directly to the Intensive Care Unit where the wife was hospitalized and where her husband greeted me with tears and what appeared to be an earnest endeavor for the authorities to reach satisfactory conclusion about the attack in its unfolding drama.

As the nature of the crime unfolds, authorities become more clear on each phase pf the drama. What appeared to give the husband more freedom, the evidence seemed more and more that he may have been involved to some extent. In the later days of gathering evidence, the police department began to focus on the daily activities of the husband. Where was he when he was making all those cell phone calls? Did he remain at the library at Perkins Seminary as long as he said he had? Evidence was growing against him. The pastor claimed that he received a threatening letter, slipped under his office door. Later it was revealed that the letter had been written from one of the church offices. Most of the positives in seeking his innocence backfired.

The pastor was a brilliant pulpitur, but a negative image began to grow on him, and his flower lost its bloom. The pastor was able to hire a well-known defense attorney, and he was successful in a change of location for the trial, from Dallas to San Antonio, Texas where the pastor was acquitted.

The one time our Bishop and the pastor ever met was after the pastor had been sent to Timberlawn Hospital to receive proper treatment. The Bishop went to visit him with a specific request – "Please turn in your ministerial credentials!"

CHAPTER 49

Early Retirement Years

I retired from the North Texas Conference of the United Methodist Church in June of 1990, having announced my intention to retire in February of that year. I choose not to reveal the circumstances involved in my choosing to retire, but the evidence can be documented.

Perhaps two weeks after I made my announcement, I was approached by the pastor of Custer Road United Methodist Church in Plano, inquiring as to whether or not I would be interested in joining the staff of that church. I responded that I would not be interested at that time but thanked him for asking me. Two weeks later, this pastor came to see me again and asked if I had been considering it. I told him again that I was not interested.

Another two weeks later, the same pastor approached me with his hand raised, palm facing me. He said, "Do not say a word! I have a proposition you cannot refuse!" Since the earlier visit, I had begun to think that it may be good for me to work part-time somewhere, perhaps even at Custer Road.

His proposition sounded something like this: "Look, I want you to make eight calls a week. You may take them to breakfast, lunch, or dinner or play golf with them, as long as you make eight calls a week. If eight calls are too many, make five." This proposition sounded rather appealing, so I said, "You have talked me into it." He then said that I had pleased him a great deal.

Two weeks later, he came to see me again. I said, "I have already told you that I would come to work in June. What now?" In his own persistent manner, he said, "Look, I have an associate who would like to take a sabbatical next January, February, and March. Would you even consider working in her place for those three months?" I thought, *These are winter months, I will not be playing much golf, and besides, we will not be traveling that much in the winter.* So I said, "Sure, I will be glad to do that!"

He smiled graciously and said, "That is wonderful!" I thought surely the visits were over this time. Wrong! Two weeks later, he came back and said, "Look!" (His favorite phrase.) "I would like to take a sabbatical in June, July, and August. Would you consider working for me while I am gone?" I said, "Why not? Sure!" He smiled broadly and said, "But I am going to pay you!" I said, "Yes, I think you will pay me well!" The deal was cut in February for me to begin working on the first of June 1990.

In retrospect, I could not have been happier. As it turned out, it became one the most rewarding positions I had ever had. What would I have done were it not for Custer Road? Jane and I left for a while and attended other churches, but it was never the same. So we decided to return there, and we will be there until God calls us home!

But this is not the end of the story. Some of the great moments in my ministry have come with the congregation of Custer Road. Let me share with you a few of these landmark memories. Our first Sunday at Custer Road coincided with the grand opening of the new sanctuary. We helped open the doors to a beautiful and functional facility that has served thousands and thousands of worshippers over the past twenty-eight years.

I cannot not tell you how many weddings I have conducted there or how many memorial services I have presided over. This is not a secret, but the pastor then was not inclined to preside over weddings or memorial services. To his credit, he would say to me whenever an opportunity arose, "Look, I would appreciate it if you would conduct (whichever), but if you need me to say a word, just let me know and I will be there to support you." He did not mention this in February before I said yes, but that was his standard remark after I took on the responsibility.

We had not been at Custer Road very long when the pastor came to me and said, "We are planning to build a chapel adjacent to the sanctuary." A couple in the church had offered to donate the funds whenever we were ready to begin. Then he said, "Do you mind taking on the project of selling their donated home located in Tanglewood Resort at Lake Texoma? (Sound familiar?) I replied, "I would be glad to if the donors do not object." He said, "I have already talked to them about it, and they would be pleased."

So a few days later, I went to Tanglewood with Joe and Doris Sowell to look at their beautiful home that would soon fund the chapel at Custer Road. After assuming the responsibility of marketing their home, I contacted all of the Realtors I could locate in the Tanglewood area and set up meetings with them so they could see the property and so I could share with them the price for the home that the Sowells had suggested.

On the day the Realtors were supposed to meet, I arrived at the home perhaps an hour early in order to properly receive them upon their arrival. Within a few minutes of my arrival, an automobile pulled up in front of the home, and a tall, stately lady came up the walk, rang the doorbell, and said that she was interested in purchasing the home at the listed price with *cash*! Needless to say, the Realtors never met, and I went back to Plano with a smile.

It was then that I realized an old cliché was true. The difference between a long, skinny girl and a tall, stately girl was three hundred thousand dollars in cash (a stately girl was one of tremendous resources)!

Custer Road took root in my heart and life quickly. I felt entirely at home, and the people were accepting and friendly. After almost thirty years, the people have come and gone, and some have aged and mellowed, but it is still home to Jane and me.

The church, in our time, has changed dramatically—and generally but not necessarily for the best. Culture is the modern change agent where the Bible once was. It seems that if anything changes, it is usually for the worse. (Pessimism sometimes rules). I look back over sixty-one years of ministry, and the future does not shape up with any clear optimism.

Custer Road stepped up to the plate several years ago when it invested in the seventeen acres on the corner of Custer Road and Legacy. The plot has proved its value over and over. As I remember it, Custer Road paid approximately one million dollars for the property, and it has served many purposes since. When the property was purchased, the pastor played magician with the City of Plano by offering them the east end of the property for a soccer field in exchange for never having to pay taxes on the totality of the property. History will record that deal as one of the finest ever made. Beyond that, the pastor had added to the contract that if the church ever needed the soccer field for further ministry development, the no-tax clause would remain in effect. The church has used the land for many purposes that would have been difficult to find other land for in close proximity to the church.

Into every good deal goes questionable consideration. It is one I have second-guessed many times. Back in about 1997, Dr. Ron DelBene, Jane's primary consultant on the Prayer Ministry Project and one of her instructors at the Spiritual Academy in Nashville, was asked to fly into DFW Airport to be part of an all-day meeting with the pastor, Jane, and me to present to us a proposal for multipurpose usage of the seventeen acres, including things like a senior activities center and other ministry buildings, plus parking, to supplement the worship facilities that presently adorn our southern campus. A great deal of pros and cons were discussed, but it sounded terrific.

After hours of exhaustive discussion, the three of us were on our way back to the church property when the pastor indicated that he wanted no part of it. That killed the whole idea. One of the intriguing questions that has occupied a portion of my brain all these years is, what if we had decided to recommend it? Would it have been a good idea or poor judgment? Time always poses stimulating questions. I am a gambler, in a way, and I saw great possibilities when others saw stumbling blocks. I am willing to take risks where others play it safe. That is why there is so much diversity in the world. This was not a right or wrong decision; it was simply an opportunity to do something different. The richness of Custer Road's great programs and ministries lies in what has happened, not in what might have happened. In either case, you and I are richer.

But the questions that all of us must answer are, What do we do next? How faithful are we now? How can we preserve our heritage? How can we prepare for an unknown future? We are an aging congregation, and the question for me is, what can I do to give the best of myself in the time I have remaining? Experience, maturity, and decisiveness trump inexperience, immaturity, and indecisiveness every day of the week.

Retirement is not for everyone! Count your blessings, and follow the Lord in all things!

CHAPTER 50

Greatest Surprise

My ministry has been filled with many different expectations—some of them realistic, some unrealistic, many ambiguous, but most of them affirming and encouraging. Through all of them, I have been challenged to fulfill my responsibilities with honor and dignity. I admit I have been diligent about those things that were challenging and difficult and were best for my congregations.

As a receiver of surprises, I have often been skeptical and somewhat embarrassed by most. However, one surprise has surpassed them all. I shall never forget a call from the pastor of a church where I had been volunteering for the previous nine years, offering my talents and experience whenever and wherever I was called upon. I was asked to meet with a designated group of laypersons, along with the pastor. I was not given a reason or a duty, simply an invitation. I thought I had been invited to, perhaps, a work session, simply as a courtesy considering my role as a volunteer professional. Boy, was I wrong!

For months, we had been working on the concept of building a family life center that would serve multiple functions. We had been through a dozen or more phases of discussion and planning for the mixed-use facility. We had also conducted a stewardship campaign through which the building would be financed and paid for. But never had I dreamed of what I was about to experience.

After much discussion about the details, the pastor, John Mollett, directed his remarks to me, saying, "We have decided to name the structure the Robertson Family Life Center."

I was absolutely stunned! Words were hard to come by. At first, I could not believe my ears.

My first thoughts were that I had done nothing to deserve such an honor. I was simply a volunteer, like many others, and had been delighted to share my expertise for the simple pleasure of working alongside other volunteers.

My response to the group, as far as I remember, was something like, "Usually, you name a building after someone who has offered to give a relatively large sum of money toward its construction." I was honored by the thought but honest in my response. We were talking about a beautiful building requiring a large sum of money to build, and to honor a generous donor seemed to be the most reasonable way to proceed. I was extremely flattered but pragmatic in my response. If I had been the pastor, under the circumstances, I would have been looking for Mr. Got Rocks!

But this was not the thinking of the group. I questioned their decision, but there is nothing in all of my experiences that has given me more pleasure. This was an unsolicited decision that was grace upon grace.

I spent nine of the most gratifying years of my ministry in retirement at Stonebridge United Methodist Church in McKinney. As director of church development, I bought the land on which this church is located. (I am not absolute about this, but my memory seems to validate it.)

Jane and I started going there while the congregation was meeting in a school. When the new sanctuary opened, with the consent of the pastor, I went on staff as a volunteer and served in several capacities for nine years.

While there, I offered the pastoral prayer every Sunday. I later had the prayers placed in a book titled *Prayers for the Pew*. I did signings at all of my former pastorates, as well as the senior residence where I live. The book can still be ordered from Amazon.

I will always be grateful to Stonebridge Church for their hospitality and generosity. To honor one's name is to honor you. No greater honor has ever been bestowed upon me!

CHAPTER 51

Mission Work

After I retired from active responsibility within my annual conference, my wife and I decided to become involved with a mission group out of Cedar Rapids, Iowa who had a reputation for serving mission projects in several areas across the Southern parts of the United States. The primary objective was constructing or rehabbing facilities that served the indigent population, mostly of ethnic origins. For three consecutive winters Jane and I signed up in this work and traveled to three different regions across the Southern parts of the U.S.

Missioners would come from several different locations within the continental United States to provide the labor and knowledge to do what each mission project required. There was generally a "foreman" for each project who was especially skilled to do whatever the project demanded. Most of the workers were experienced in one or more of the required skills to complete the task the group had accepted. My father was a carpenter and I had worked on numerous jobs with him and had become basically knowledgeable about what goes into a given project.

The missioners all drove pick-up trucks with either a "bumper-pull" house trailer or a "5th Wheel hitch mounted on the back of their pick-ups, to provide them suitable housing on each site.

So, for Jane and me, our first decision was to purchase a pick-up and to decide what kind of trailer we were going to buy. This was going to be a challenge because I had never owned a pick-up. As I thought about buying a pick-up, I remembered a commercial I had heard on the radio many times. A Mr. Lewis from Canton, Texas had an ad that was very appealing to me that went something like this: "If you are interested in buying a pick-up, I will meet you at 2:00am in the morning, if that us your desire". I thought he must be desperate if he is willing to be at his dealership at 2:00am. His volume of sales must be exceedingly low.

So, I drove from Dallas to Canton, perhaps sixty miles, to inquire from this desperate man about the purchase of a pick-up. When I arrived in Canton, I drove directly to his dealership to discover a near vacant lot, only two pick-ups were on the lot. I parked and went into the building to find Mr. Lewis. When I opened the door into his showroom there were no vehicles on the floor, only a young man of high school age sweeping the showroom floor. I asked him if I could speak to one of the salesmen, and he replied: "We only have one and that is Mr. Lewis. He is in his office with a prospective buyer. He will be with you shortly".

Within a few minutes Mr. Lewis came out dressed in blue jeans, denim shirt and work shoes. (my opinion was reinforced). I told Mr. Lewis what I was looking for and he said (what I already knew) that his inventory was low, but he could order just what I needed and have it within a couple of weeks. He quoted the price without having to lo0ok at his marketing manual. I am sure he knew precisely what the price was.

He passed the time cordially and I thanked him generously for the information and said something like: "I will get back to you soon." I left the building and drove back to Dallas feeling very sad for this poor man who needed badly to make a sale.

In the long run I finally bought a pick-up in Grand Prairie from a Ford Dealer who belonged to the Methodist church and actually let me have the pickup at cost. But not before I learned that Mr. Lewis owned several hundred acres of land, on which the Canton First Monday Trade Day, leased a number of acres from him which softened my feelings about a "must buy" from him. Mr. Lewis was doing fine with or without a sale.

After the acquisition of a pick-up, we then began to look for a trailer to pull behind it. After much consideration I decided to buy a 5th wheel trailer. After looking at the options I felt that a 5th wheel would pull more comfortably on the road.

Now we were fully equipped to travel with necessary equipment for roadside or RV Park. We made a few trial runs before we took it on the road. Everything worked smoothly and we felt we were ready to be missionaries.

Our first assignment was in Louisiana, in the suburbs of Lake Charles. I do not remember the project, but it was more of the same. However, I do remember the crew who were there to work. What a hospitable bunch they were! They made us feel welcome and needed. We had a marvelous time of fellowship and worship. The project was more "fix-it-up" but we enjoyed the people so much. Part of the project was during Mardi Gras. The floats were beautifully decorated, and the festivities were fabulous. One of our Methodist agencies UMCOR had a depot there where they supplied a large region with various goods and services. It was our intension to go back and work in the depot, but time and circumstances prevented it.

Arizona Project

Our next visit was a year away, but we travelled to Southern Arizona, near the border of Old Mexico and spent several days in the heat. The work was warm and dusty, but we thoroughly enjoyed it all.

We were in Southeastern Arizona near Bisbee, about ten miles from Old Mexico. The work was not as deliberate as it was in Louisiana and not near as demanding as it will be when we go to Florida. But we were able to complete our assignment in a few days, which gave us time to visit some historic places as well as cross the border for a few hours.

One of the highlights of our trip was a visit to the old west town of Tombstone, of Wyatt Earp fame. The town is ghost-like, but the characters came to life in the famous shoot-out with the Clanton gang.

A memorable afternoon was spent in the Tombstone cemetery. One could walk the entire area and enjoy the poetry on the tombstones and relive the names and faces it brought to mind. I remember vividly a "catchy" little epitaph on one of the stones.

Here lies Lester Moore
Dead from the slugs of a forty-four
No Les – No more!

Florida Project

The third-year project was by far the best, but one that called forth our very best skills. The project was perhaps twenty miles from Disney World. The project was most unusual. It was a complete leveling of a home that had been destroyed by termites. One could walk carefully throughout the house where all the floors were sagging badly because the termites had destroyed the entire foundation.

The home was occupied by a single woman perhaps in her 70's or 80's. All the furniture was riddled by termites, so much so that you could not pick up a piece of furniture without the thing crumbling to pieces.

Our task was to give the home a rebuilt foundation room by room. There was a time in the beginning when we literally met as a group to decide how this project could be carried out.

Our decision was to begin in the kitchen. We tore the entire floor out and started in one corner with new floor joints, making sure that everything was square, with new concrete pillars in all four corners with several scattered around through the breadth and width of the room. We used concrete bricks to insure the stability of the construction. Once we replaced the floor everything was plumb and square and stable. Once we put the new floor down, the room seemed good as new.

The we went from room to room repeating what we had done in the kitchen, making sure everything was supported by a strong foundation and that it was square and stable.

One of the problems was trying to move the furniture I n each room. It was impossible. The termites had literally destroyed the entire house, furniture and everything. This was tedious work and it took what seemed forever for us to do the whole house. Perhaps it should have been destroyed and completely rebuilt but the occupant lived in the house all the while we were reconstructing it.

When we finally finished, difficult though it was, we felt pride in our work and the lady who lived there was so gracious in her gratitude.

On completion of our work, the entire house was "tented" from roof to ground and it went through a complete termite treatment. We were told that the termites could return and ruin the structure again, but it could last the remainder of the occupant's days.

CHAPTER 52

Honor Flight 25 to Washington, DC, 2015

I was invited to go on Honor Flight 25 from Dallas-Fort Worth to Washington, DC as a veteran of the Korean War, a two-day event in June 2015. I was required to take someone with me as a companion to look out after my personal needs, and my oldest son, Stephen, was a willing and able assistant.

We flew from DFW on Friday, June 12, and returned on Saturday, June 13, a whirlwind trip in which we visited all of the military and most of the national historic monuments in Washington, DC. Some of the major attractions were the Washington Monument, the Lincoln Memorial, the World War II Memorial, the Korean Memorial, the Air Force Memorial, and the Iwo Jima Memorial, along with a stop at Arlington National Cemetery.

When we visited the Arlington National Cemetery, we went by the tomb of America's most decorated WWII soldier, Audie Murphy. As we approached his place of burial, our guide asked each of us to be prepared to place a quarter on top of his headstone without giving an explanation. After we had followed his request, the guide shared that Audie's nickname had been Two-bits. None of us had ever heard the story.

I experienced a most unique event on the Friday evening we visited the Naval Museum. As we entered the museum, my son and I didn't know exactly where we were to go. We saw a room full of people, and I assumed it was the place assigned for our visit.

After entering the large room, we noticed a naval officer at the front of the room in a receiving line. We quickly assumed that we were in the wrong place and turned to exit the room when an older man approached me. I had on a naval cap with the name of my former ship, the *USS Helena* (CA-75), printed at the top of my cap above the bill. The man looked at me and then at my cap, and he said, "Were you once aboard the *USS Helena*?"

I said that I was. He turned toward the naval officer in the reception line and said, "Don, come here, quick!" Of course, the officer did not come because he was in the receiving line. The man I was talking to was the officer's father. In a very few seconds, the father said to his son, "Don, come right here right now!"

The officer immediately left the receiving line and came to where we were standing. When he arrived, he took one look at my cap and one look at me and said, "Were you aboard the *Helena*?" I responded that I was. Then, to my utter surprise, he said, "I am the retiring commander of the *USS Helena*, which is now a nuclear submarine."

I must say how surprised I was because, when I was aboard the *Helena*, it was a heavy cruiser named after the capital city of Helena, Montana. My ship was cut up into scrap metal in the mid-1960s. Little did I know that the nomenclature after which ships were named had changed sometime long after I was discharged. When I was in the service, one could always determine the type of ship by its name. For example, battleships were named after states, aircraft carriers were named after famous battles, and submarines were named after fish. (The US Department of Defense will do whatever it wants without asking former navy personnel for permission.)

We also visited one of the air force bases in the Washington, DC area, and when we arrived, several of the top officers of the base were on hand to greet us and to escort us into a large auditorium, where we were greeted and entertained by perhaps the top orchestra related to the air force. Female servicepeople were on hand to dance with the "old veterans." It was quite an evening.

We were then taken to the airport for our return trip home, exhausted from our whirlwind trip. Upon boarding the plane, there was a "mail call" during which each veteran was given a sack of mail from their family and friends back home. I will never forget the letters I received thanking me for my military service. It has been three years since the event, but it has made a permanent impression on my life.

CHAPTER 53

Return to Korea

In June 2017, I was invited by the Korean Veteran's Association, along with perhaps twenty or so others who had served in the military during the Korean conflict between 1950-1952. I was thrilled to receive an invitation, so I filled in the application and mailed it in as directed. We were told that it would be necessary for me to be accompanied by an adult family member or friend. I contacted my daughter, Lori and she readily agreed to accompany me.

We made our reservation to fly out of the DFW airport on the given date, flying Korean Airlines direct from Dallas-Ft. Worth to Seoul, Korea. The flight took approximately twelve hours. My daughter and I were the only Caucasians on the flight, the rest of the passengers were foreign nationals. The flight was long and without incident.

The airport serving Seoul was located on an island west of the mainland at the port on Incheon. It was a magnificent and ultra-modern airport, the likes of which I had never seen. Once we had arrived, there were messengers waiting at our gate to instruct us where we would be able to catch our bus that would take us into Seoul. The airport was an experience all its own. It made DFW look small and in some ways ill equipped, but we followed directions and located our bus.

The trip from the airport to our hotel was an education all its own. It was perhaps 30 miles or more from the airport to our hotel. After we had driven onto the mainland, the topography revealed a slight mountain range covered with trees to our left, and on the right side of the bus we could see well groomed farmland, where periodically we would see three or four slender high rises grouped together where people loved, along with two or more green houses were situated every once in a while where the farmers would grow food for the people to eat.

We were told that South Korea has a population of roughly 55,000,000 and that the country grows and feeds the entire population without importing food products. I found this to be astounding!

As we continued into Seoul, which has a resident population of approximately 25,000,000 we saw many other apartment house complexes. With three or four high-rises in acreage here and another three or four high rises a mile or so away. I do not remember seeing a single-family home between the airport and Seoul.

The skyline became more dense as we became closer to the city. One could tell that urban planning had occurred and they had been extremely successful in planning the metropolitan area. All of the shopping centers were not necessarily obvious, but you had the assurances that the Korean people had planned carefully and well. A nation of high rises accommodates residents as well as business needs.

We arrived in what I suspected was downtown Seoul, there were some visible signs that marked certain areas and buildings. We were taken to our hotel the Grand Ambassador where we off-loaded, given keys to our rooms and told that we would only be there one night. The next morning, we were to store our primary luggage and take smaller bags to board busses the next morning to visit some of the battlefields and other sights on our way to the DMZ.

Day 1

We had a wonderful breakfast at the Grand Ambassador before we checked out and began our excursion of visiting some of the battle sites such as Heartbreak Ridge and Bloody Ridge, after a box lunch on the bus we visited the Punchbowl and the Eulchi Observatory. After an exhausting day we spent the night at the Hantan River Spa hotel in Cheorwon. We had spent an exhausting day visiting and reliving some of the extreme conditions that our troops faced.

Day 2

One of the highlights of this day was a visit to Infiltration Tunnel #4 that had been dug by the North Koreans. Since 1974 there have been 4 tunnels crossing the DMZ. North Korea claimed that the tunnels were for coal mining; however, no coal was found in the tunnels, which were dug through granite. Some of the tunnel walls were painted black to give the appearance of anthracite. The tunnels are believed to have been planned as a military invasion route by North Korea. Following each tunnel discovery, engineering within the tunnels became progressively more advanced. The 4th tunnel was discovered on March 3, 1990, North of Haean town in the former Punchbowl battlefield. The soldiers had dug by hand using dynamite to the height of 5'7 which was the average height of the North Korean soldiers. The tunnel is approximately 476' deep. We rode a small electric train for perhaps 200' or more into the mountain to give us a feeling of what had happened.

Day 3

We visited the North Korean's Workers Party Headquarters building and had lunch in Cheorwon. In the afternoon we visited the Key (Yolsei) Observatory to view the T-Bone Battlefield, White Horse Hill and the Old Baldy battlefield.

Day 4

We got to visit the Peace (Pyonghwa) Observatory and drive through the countryside. As we were driving you could look on either side of the road and see these red and yellow triangular signs that said "Mine" danger. They are still clearing some of these areas today but will take many years. We also got to see a lot of agriculture. The main crops are Ginseng and rice. Cheorwon is known for its spectacular rice. At the observatory we were instructed not to take any pictures or point our camera's toward North Korea. Anyone found to be doing this would have their camera taken away. You could step outside of the observatory on one side and hear broadcasted propaganda being blasted from North Korea into South Korea. If you went out the door on the opposite side of the building, you could hear propaganda being blasted from South Korean into North Korea. We were told that from 1953 until 2004 both sides broadcast audio propaganda across the DMZ. Massive loudspeakers mounted on several of the buildings delivered DPRK propaganda broadcasts directed towards the South as well as propaganda radio broadcasts across the border. In 2004 the North and South agreed to end the broadcasts.

In 2015, a border incident occurred where two South Korean soldiers were wounded after stepping on landmines that had 'allegedly' been laid on the southern side of the DMZ by North Korean forces near an ROK guard post. When this happened both sides then resumed broadcasting propaganda by loudspeaker. After short negotiations both agreed to end the broadcasts.

On January 8, 2016 in response to North Korea's supposed successful testing of a hydrogen bomb, South Korea resumed broadcasts directed at the North.

Both North and South Korea have also used balloon propaganda since the Korean War. In addition to using balloons as a means of delivery, North Koreans have also used rockets to send leaflets to the DMZ.

On April 23, 2018, both North and South Korea officially cancelled their border propaganda broadcasts for the last time.

Day 5

We drove the 30 miles or so to the DMZ (Korean Demilitarized Zone). The DMZ is 160 miles long and approximately 2.5 miles wide. Though the zone is demilitarized, the border beyond that strip is one of the most heavily militarized borders in the world.

In the Armistice Agreement of July 1953, the DMZ was created as each side agreed to move their troops back 1.2 miles from the front line, creating a buffer zone 2.5 miles wide. The MDL (Military Demarcation Line) goes through the center of the DMZ and indicates where the front was when the agreement was signed. Due to the genuine hostility between North and South Korea, large numbers of troops are stationed along both sides of the line, each side guarding against potential aggression from the other side, even 66 years after its establishment. The JSA (Joint Security Area) is located here at the DMZ. The JSA is the location where all negotiations since 1953 have been held. The MDL goes through the conference rooms and down the middle of the conference tables where the North Koreans and the United Nations meet face to face.

We were allowed to go inside the main conference room where these meetings and negotiations are held. Before we were allowed to leave our bus, we were told that if we saw any North Korean soldiers, we were not to make any hand movements or speak to them. They instructed us that this could be construed as a want to defect into North Korea. While we were there, we only saw one North Korean soldier who was stationed outside the North Korean Panmungak (Panmun Hall) and was facing towards the South. Alongside of each of the JSA buildings were South Korean soldiers who were all facing north. It was a very strange feeling to go inside this conference room and be at the JSA after seeing this exact same thing on the news for so long.

Another very interesting sight was seeing the "Propaganda Village". It was the North Korean 'Peace" village also called Kijong-dong. The town features a number of brightly painted, poured-concrete multi-story buildings and apartments with electric lighting. These features represented an unheard-of- level of luxury for rural Koreans, North or South, in the 1950's. The town was oriented so that the bright blue roofs and whites' sides of the buildings would be the most distinguishing features when viewed from the border. However, based on scrutiny with modern telescopic lenses, it has been claimed that the buildings are mere concrete shells lacking window glass or even interior rooms, with the building lights turned on and off at set times and the empty sidewalks swept by a skeleton crew of caretakers in an effort to preserve the illusion of activity.

The rest of our trip was spent in Seoul. The days were filled with visiting sites in and around the city.

One of the highlights was a visit to the National Museum of Korea where we met a party of young Korean girls in some kind of school uniform. I judged them to be 8-10 years old. My daughter had brought some Texas souvenirs to pass on by choice at various places. She handed me a couple of Dallas Cowboy stickers and said "Dad, why don't you give these to one of the girls" that was in a group of five of six. I chose the smallest of the girls to whom I would given the stickers. When I handed it to her, she looked at it for several perspectives before exclaiming" Oh, the Dallas Cowboys! My dad's favorite team". She gave me a big hug and thanked me for the present.

We were bussed over for a huge 67th Year celebrating the Korean War. This was held at the Seoul Olympic stadium where the 1988 Summer Olympic Games were held. Our busses were escorted by police both in car and motorcycle. There were dignitaries from both the US and South Korea including the South Korean President Park Geun-hye. We were entertained with musical performances, war enactments and a military martial arts performance. It was a very moving experience. We each had earpieces which handled the language translation for us.

We visited the Seoul National Cemetery which was beautiful. Engraved inside the memorial are the memorial tablets of 104,000 fallen soldiers of the Korean War whose remains could not be found. There was a very spiritual ceremony held for us which was so moving.

The last but most exciting event was a beautiful "Thank You" banquet hosted by the MPVA and KVA in the Grand ballroom of the Ambassador Hotel. As luck would have it, I had been chosen to sit at the head table with several dignitaries. I was there early and shortly after a tall military office and his wife came in and sat next to me. He was a man of high rank. After a while I said to him: "General if I may be permitted, what is your assignment?" He responded by saying: "I am in command of all allied forces in the far East." My heart quickly jumped to my throat as I realized I was sitting next to what would have been Douglas MacArthur as generation or two ago. What a high privilege it was to be in such high company. His name was General Vincent Brooks, a four-star general, wow! I had my picture taken with him and his wife.

There were several welcome speeches and each veteran was presented with an Ambassador of Peace medal. A magnificent gold medal with a ribbon that went around the neck. I will forever treasure this significant honor.

This act brought to close our banquet and in a real way our visit to Seoul and South Korea. I will forever treasure this trip as one of my finest ever. The South Korean's were a genuinely friendly people and their hospitality ranks in the highest digit.

Our return trip home was long and tiring but will rank exceedingly high on my world travels.

CHAPTER 54

Golf: A Minister's Respite

There is an old cliché: "All work and no play makes Jack a dull boy!" Most ministers I know work an inordinate amount of time and are under an inordinate amount of pressure, therefore needing a respite. For me, that respite was golf. I was good enough to enjoy the competition but not good enough to think of being on the PGA Tour. On my best days, I have shot par. On my worst days, I thought about taking up water polo or wrestling alligators.

A respite is a time-out. When the pressures of life begin to close in upon us, we need to be able to open the petcock and let a little steam escape. Life has a way of closing in upon us, and we need to find a way to unwind, relax, and debrief. A respite never puts more pressure upon us; rather, it is something like a soothing massage with a few bumps and bruises.

In one of my appointments, I was superintendent of a given district. The district parsonage was located on the first fairway of a city-owned and operated golf course. My fellow players and I maintained a regular schedule of playing every Thursday, weather permitting. I always looked forward to the great fellowship we enjoyed and to a splendid round of golf, regardless of the score. I have been playing golf for over sixty years and have enjoyed the game immensely. One does not have to score well to enjoy the game, but scoring well enhances the enjoyment.

My regular partner had a way of talking to himself, and when I asked him why he did so, he had a stock answer: "Because I like talking to a smart man, and I like to hear a smart man talk!"

On a particular day, I scheduled a district golf outing and invited anyone and everyone who served in my district. We must have had thirty to thirty-five golfers mulling around the clubhouse waiting for our tee times. I decided to stroll out to the parking lot to see if we had any late arrivals when I noticed one of my district ministers getting out of his car. He was impeccably dressed in dark slacks, a beautifully tailored dress shirt, and freshly shined alligator loafers, heading for the clubhouse. I asked him if he had come to play golf, and he said that he had. I reminded him to retrieve his golf clubs, but he informed me that he did not have any. I foolishly reminded him to put on his golf shoes, but he said he did not have any golf shoes either. Golf balls? No!

I escorted him into the golf shop, rented him a set of clubs, and bought him a few golf balls and a new golf glove. I felt, under the conditions that was about all I could do for him. He had never before played the game and obviously knew little about the equipment needed for the outing, but he was terrifically excited about being there. I placed him into a foursome and tried to stay as far away from him as I could until the round was over. I am not sure if I ever saw his foursome again, but from that day on he became an avid fan of the game and later the first African-American pastor of Custer Road United Methodist Church.

I have had the good fortune to play some of the top golf courses known to mankind. Along with one of my sons, we played a course in Switzerland where the Swiss Open was played. I cannot remember the name of the course, but I do know that the measurement was laid out in meters instead of yards. I was totally unaware of that, and to my knowledge, I drove over every green (no doubt because of the altitude), to the chagrin of the foursome ahead of us. You would have thought that a man of my knowledge and skill would have figured that out before we finished eighteen holes. I must have had a double portion of Wheaties that morning and later thought how impressive I was at driving the golf ball so far.

I also played Old St. Andrews on a trip to Northern Scotland. I thought someone had posted the wrong yardage on most of the holes, and I spent my quota of strokes trying to blast out of the pot bunkers. My caddy quit before my round was over, but I endured to the end.

I was most fortunate to have been invited to play in two of the Byron Nelson Pro-Ams. I am sure that there could have been many other courses, including the Dallas Country Club, the Dallas National, Stonebridge Ranch and Dye Courses, several courses in the Hawaiian Islands, where the Swiss Open is played, and others of renown.

At my age now, golf is still fun but double the pleasure (if you know what I mean).

Recreation is nothing less or more than 're-creation.' Everyone needs a little diversion in their life.

I played my first round of golf when I was about 21 or 22 years of age. A game that looked relatively simple and perhaps on the side of easy, was exceedingly tough. After all the clubs were designed for a particular distance, give or take a few yards if properly hit. The dimpled ball looked innocent enough, round and hard, nut a mishit can send one offline several yards, perhaps into a hazard.

After my first round I was greatly humiliated. How difficult can this game be? A club, a ball, a given distance, a swing and bingo, something different happened every time. This can't be! I grew up playing baseball through high school and was good enough to earn my spot on the field and at bat. With baseball, the equipment was essentially the same, but with golf every shot required something unique, perhaps a different club, perhaps a full or partial swing, always demanding something I seemed not to have.

But the challenge to do better seemed to motivate me more. I know I can do this, but why don't I? Golf was a challenge to my mind and muscles. I can do this, but why do I struggle so much? There were days and days of little or no improvement. I generally played with those of my own skill level. Who else would play with me? Perhaps golf is a competition of those persons who play on my own skill level. But why is my skill level not improving? Do I need to p lay with someone more gifted or skilled? But who would want to play with me as long as I scored in three digits? I thought about quit trying to play golf and go back to another sport, but I was haunted by the fact that I wasn't getting better and somehow something inside me said 'you can! You can!'

The cost of playing golf seemed to discourage me. I was a low-income person who was spending more than I was capable, but the challenge was driving me to improve. At my salary level I often sought 'driving ranges' and less expensive golf courses. How many years, how many rounds of golf will it take for me to compete at the next level? It wasn't enough for me to equal or edge my competition, if I was still shooting in three digits. To be able to beat my brothers was rewarding and afforded me 'bragging rights', but the score had to come down. I wanted to be at least a 'two-digit' golfer.

My first break came when I was about twenty-eight years of age. The minister I was working with was three years my senior and perhaps ten strokes better per round. He invited me to begin playing with him and two other clergy golfers on a weekly basis, on the municipal golf courses within the Dallas area. We normally played the Tenison Golf course in East Dallas. It was a good, but tough layout. There were no tee times by phone. The way you worked your way up to 'tee-off' was that when you arrived at the course, one of your four-some would place a ball in a triangular rack at the first hole. As the foursome teed off your ball would roll closer to the tee. When your ball was first to the end of the Eagle iron, your tee-time had arrived. Normally we would wait fifteen to thirty minutes before we could tee off. There were no electric carts on Tenison, so everyone walked which made it equal for all. Our rounds would normally last four hours or more, nut within a satisfactory time frame.

Dallas had several public golf courses, including Cedar Crest, Stephens Park, L.B. Houston and some that have dropped from my memory bank. Golf became more than a 'habit', it became a desire for me to play weekly and to begin to play better. It was rare for me and my friends to ever play twice in one week. Golf was recreation not a way of life. To be employed one was to honor their work, but for good mental and physical exercise a four-hour round of golf was therapeutic.

After I left being an Associate Pastor for years, I received an appointment as pastor-in-charge, my habits never changed. I sought out pastors of other denominations and along with accompanying lay persons we generally formed a bonded four-some and played weekly on courses in nearby towns. This worked well for golf as well as building friendships and camaraderie between churches within our community. There was strong competition from both clergy and laity from the Christian community that deepened our relationships and built a more wholesome working relationship throughout the religious community.

Then in the church conference year of 1967 I was appointed back to the Dallas area to Schreiber Memorial Methodist church in North Dallas near W.T.White high school, Hockaday and what later became the Valley View shopping mall. The public golf courses were farther away, but I was fortunate to be near the Brookhaven Country Club, where I was often invited by a church member to play with them at the club.

I was invited to a new dimension of golfing. Country Club golfers were generally better than the average municipal golfers. A special friend, Bill Stewart frequently invited me to play with him at Brookhaven. Bill was better than I was, and he enjoyed the longer course at Brookhaven, which I believe was the Masters, while I preferred the shorter course, which was the championship. I had not mastered the lo9ng ball as did Mr. Stewart, nor did I ever really. But if you are the beggar you play what the master plays.

I did not belong to a club at this point. My golf was still in the making. I did join a club in East Dallas, near Garland but was given a preferential clergy membership which did not charge me monthly dues. However, the golfers I played with, If I invited them to play with me, I normally paid their green fees. My golf at this club became less frequent until I resigned my membership.

While I was pastor at Schreiber there was an occasional visitor who paid for my entry into the Byron Nelson for two consecutive years, which entitled me to play in the Pro-am. This was big time for me, and I was playing far over my head. I played one year, along with four other amateurs all paired with professional golfer Bobby Watkins. This was not the most exciting outing for me. Often the Pro would hurry us up in order for us to finish a hole in time to match the other teams. On occasion the pro would ask us to pick up our balls on the green because it took too much time for some of us to putt. Instead of it being an outing where we enjoyed the pro, the pro was not enjoying 'duffer-golf' and moved us along too quickly.

Golf became different and more affordable for me after I became a District Superintendent. I could afford to invite more clergy golfers to play with me and I could sponsor District tournaments which were fun for all level of golfers, and I could arrange more foursomes whenever it was appropriate. District tournaments would allow thirty to forty participants and it was there that I shot my best golf. My scores revealed that I was a 5-6 handicapped player. Golf comes and goes and now it has gone. I miss the disciplined exercise; I miss the camaraderie you got on a golf course. Golfers are a breed of their own and I am one of them.

Golf is more than a game; it is a commentary of the way you live. Golf is played accordingly to the riles of the game. One cannot break the rules and play fairly or honesty. Golf is a framework which operates within its own parameters. You either play at golf or you play golf. There are no substitutions for the real thing. The rules of golf cannot be broken. They can only be disobeyed. To disobey is to leave the arena which golf is played and to accept the rules of our own making.

One cannot cheat at golf – for cheating is a basic flaw from taking the rules seriously and flawlessly. One is made complete by adhering to the rules. To be true to golf is to be obedient in every aspect.

CHAPTER 55

Famed Stories from Creede

Winters come and go, but Creede, Colorado remains!

Creede, Colorado an old mining town lingers still in the mountains of Southern Colorado just a "hoot and a hollow" North of Wolf Creek Pass. The narrow-gauge railroad tracks hints of a silver mining ages ago. The town boasts of a population of 500 sturdy residents who hold the community together and provides the near ideal summer weather that enhances tourism. The repertory theater is perhaps second to none.

Creede is a gentle town supporting one grocery store, one service station, one hotel, one mobile home park as well as one cemetery. Creede is the only township in Mineral County. A few years ago, a group of developers approached the town council concerning an interest in building a huge ski resort in close proximity to Wolf Creek Pass which would bring thousands to ski the slopes of Wolf Creek and bring real estate development to the area. The town council quickly vetoed the proposition and thus the township maintains the "one of everything" in types of business and approximately 500 persons on the steamship.

Creede has many stories, but my favorite are the two I am about to share with you.

The first story involves the infamous Jesse James gang who had plundered the railroad and other monopolies and had extracted plenty of money. Jesse James had retired and was living under the assumed name of Mr. Howard, a peaceful citizen although there was a reward posted on the infamous Jesse James. Story has it that Bob Ford shot Mr. Howard through a window in his home while he was attempting to hang a picture with his back to the infamous villain. Upon the murder of Mr. Howard, Bob Ford fled Missouri and went to Creede, Colorado and there he opened a saloon and gambling joint.

The town folk in Missouri were so in sensed that Jesse James had been killed they in turn hired a man to go to Creede and murder Bob Ford. The assassin carries out his duty. The townsfolk of Creede were in sympathy with their counterparts in Missouri, wo much to they would not allow Bob Ford to be buried in the city cemetery of Creede. To find Bob Fords grave, one has to search the remote area of Creede to find a place to bury Bob Ford. So today there is a grave that holds Bob Fords body, but it is far removed from the town cemetery. Bob Ford is totally alone in a grave removed from any of the other citizens.

The second story concerns a hunting party from Creede that went hunting in the mountains during the winter and found themselves trapped in a cave in the higher regions. A winter storm had turned worse and the men froze to death except one man. In order for him to preserve his own life he was forced to eat the flesh of the other men with him who had died. When he was finally rescued from the cold, it was discovered that he had eaten the last Democrat in Mineral County!

CHAPTER 56

Journey Through Ministry

A friend of mine gave me a small, but significant book, by the title of "The Butterfly Effect". I read the book over and over again and wondered if the theory posed by the author had any validity. In fact, the author presented his theory to a science board in New York State and they declared there was no evidence to give him credibility.

Thirty years later (1993) a group of scientists declared that the theory was sound in principle if not in actual demonstration. An idea, if constantly reinforced, can be true to the premise if one is following a singular thought pattern.

I want to show with my reader exactly how I was influenced by a singular event that was reinforced many times over.

On July 9, 1948 I was planning to join the U.S. Navy the very next day, which was my eighteenth birthday. To enlist one had to be eighteen. I was home with my mother when she said to me: "Pete, I want you to make me a promise." I said: "What is it mother?" She said: "I want you to promise me that you will not come home from the military like your brothers did from World War II." I said to her: "Mother, I promise!"

For the first time in my life I felt the flapping of butterfly wings! I felt that a significant force had gripped my life, that I had been bound to my mother's wishes in a profound way that I would never forget and that I would after circumstances to be sure that I was faithful to it. I felt the flapping of Butterfly Wings!

My mother was very precious to me, so much so, that I was willing to bond herself to mine, and that I would be true to my promise. In a real way my mother was God to me in those moments and that I had entered into a covenant which I would honor.

I know there were many times during my Navy career that my mother would have disapproved of my attitude and my actions, but her admonition was, that you will not come home like this! What she meant was that I would come home with a given discipline and resolve to live a life becoming a mature man possessed by the qualities of a Christian gentleman.

So, I have strung together a few vignettes that I think are important to demonstrate how I tried to be true to the promise I made to my mother. (My mother was the best representative of God that I knew – so in a way a promise to her was a promise to God).

Now let me fast-forward my life almost four years later. My ship was returning from Korean waters after my second deployment. The time was near for me to be discharged from the service. I had married after our return from Korea. So, before I was transferred to the Separation Center, I sent my wife, by bus, to Apache Junction, Arizona to stay with her parents until I could join her after my discharge.

When I received my discharge papers, along with my very best friend, we went to the nearest tavern and ordered a beer for our final drink together. I consumed about half of mine, when I scooted it back. I said to my friend: "That's it! I promised my mother." It may seem like a small incidental thing, but to me it was the keeping of a promise I had made almost four years earlier. Now sixty-seven years have passed without a single drop of beer.

After a brief visit with my wife's family, we boarded a bus for Texas and home! When we arrived in Plains, Texas, where one of my brothers lived, he and his wife were waiting at the bus station. We spent a few days with them, and they were able to drive us to Dallas to see our parents. While we were in Plains my brother told me that he had applied for me a job with Shell Oil Company in a neighboring town. So on to Dallas for a few days and back out to West Texas where I would be trained to become a construction welder inside a gasoline plant. It sounded like short-term employment to me. But I needed a job and this one paid well.

On our return to Plains we visited the small Methodist church there and we joined on a profession of faith. The pastor was an older man, about the age of my father. This was the second time I felt the flapping of Butterfly Wings, a sign to me of approval.

I found a great deal of energy in joining the church and my wife and I were eager to serve in some capacity. I began teaching a class of children in Sunday school. Although my teachings had little personal depth, I was extremely gratified by the responsibility.

We became very close to the pastor and his wife as well as the Principal of the elementary school and his family. However, as our lives were being enriched by our church family, the men at my workstation began to pick at me about my newly found church experience. The workplace was becoming an adversary to my church experience. I was not mature enough to deal with both properly.

A couple of years passed with me torn in two directions without the maturity to handle it. My mother became ill in Dallas from an old disease and we decided to leave Shell and move to Seagoville, just East of Dallas, where my family lived, to be with my mother and her last days. My wife and I joined First Methodist Church in Seagoville our first Sunday there, and that evening I found myself working with the youth of the church. The Butterfly was ecstatic!

In the Spring of 1956, my mother underwent surgery to discover that her cancer had spread and there was little hope for survival after two to three months. It was then the vigil began. There were six boys in our family, and we began to take turns being by our mother's side. Mother had always stated that she wanted her six sons to be her pallbearers. On June 25, 1956 my mother passed away and her six sons bore her body to its final resting place.

Then came an awful shock, my father suffered a fatal heart attack on my mother's birthday September 12, 1956 just three short months after the death of our mother.

Again, the son's carried our dad's body to its final resting place.

My life had been under conviction concerning whether or not God was calling me into his service. The pastor of the Seagoville church had become a strong companion and was working with me to determine if I was feeling the intensity of that calling. I had felt the presence of God's spirit for months challenging me to make a decision, but I was stressed about a lack of funds to attend college, as well as a certainty of the call.

Finally, by the Fall of 1956 I was convinced that God was wooing me to surrender my life to Him. One Sunday morning during the invitation I stepped out into aisle and made my way to the altar. The pastor greeted me and said: "Why have you come?" I said: "Because I want to be a minister of Jesus Christ!" The pastor then asked me: "Do you have any reservations?" I said: "No!" but under my breath I said to God: "Lord, I am jumping this morning into something I have no idea how I am going to accomplish it. So, if I jump, you must be ready to catch me!"

My decision to become a minister required the educational requirement of a bachelor's degree and the requirement of a master's degree – both from an accredited college or university. Here I was twenty-six years old with no funds for either.

The pastor of my church was way ahead of me. He had been out to Southern Methodist University and had discussed with them the possibility of them allowing me to enroll after taking an entrance exam, with me receiving scholarship aid.

Thus, in the Spring semester of 1957, after passing the entrance exam I enrolled and began classes in January with me working 10 hours a week in the office of the Vice President of S.M.U. I could hardly believe it! My first semester I was required to pay $250.00. I worked in the V.P. office for four semesters after which I continued to pay only $250.00 a semester for my four years at S.M.U. Too good to be true but it was! After graduating from S.M.U. with a bachelor's degree in social studies, I enrolled in Perkins School of Theology on a full scholarship. I was absolutely convinced when God calls – he provides!

From the promise I made to my mother – throughout my ministry I have been affirmed by the Spirit of God working in my life. The Butterfly never stopped flapping its wings, and the miracles of God never ceased to support me.

CPSIA information can be obtained
at www.ICGtesting.com
Printed in the USA
BVHW071124160120
569728BV00004B/17/P